# Vintage Tractors

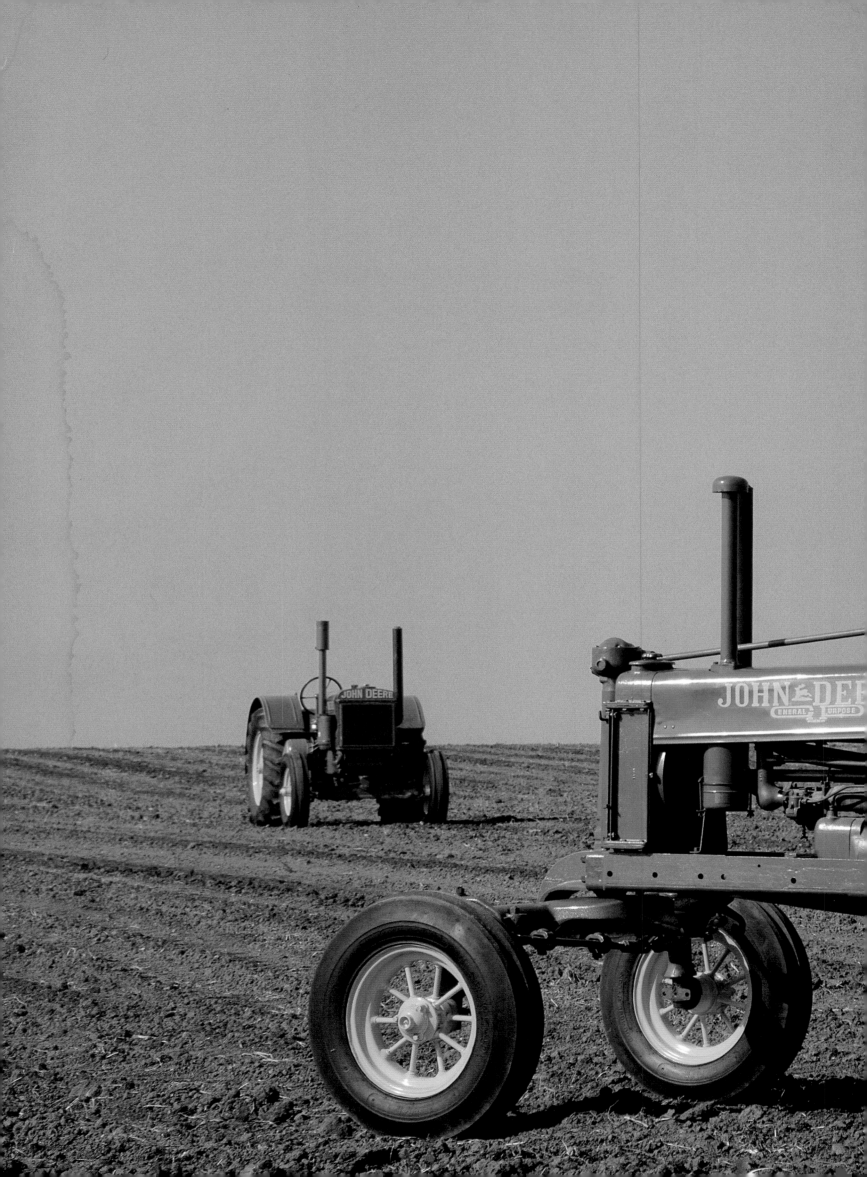

# American Rustic

# *Vintage* Tractors

### April Halberstadt

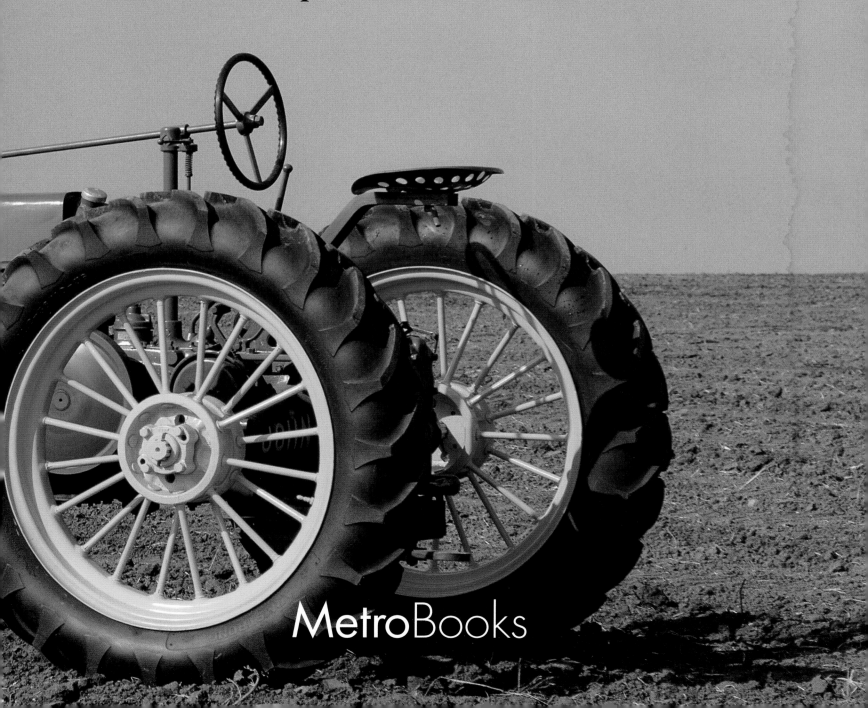

MetroBooks

# MetroBooks

An Imprint of Friedman/Fairfax Publishers

©2001 by Michael Friedman Publishing Group, Inc.

Library of Congress Cataloging-in-Publication Data available upon request.

Halberstadt, April, 1943–
   Vintage tractors / April Halberstadt.
     p.  cm. — (American rustic)
   Includes bibliographical references and index.
   ISBN 1-58663-084-9(alk. paper)
    1. Farm tractors—United States. 2. Antique and class tractors. I. Title. II. Series.

TL233.6F37 H347 2001
631.3'72'0973—dc21

00-062512


Editor: Daniel Heend
Art Director: Kevin Ullrich
Designer: Mark Weinberg
Photography Editor: Lori Epstein
Production Manager: Rosy Ngo

Color separations by Leefung-Asco Repro
Printed in China by Leefung-Asco Printers Ltd.

1  3  5  7  9  10  8  6  4  2

For bulk purchases and special sales, please contact:
Friedman/Fairfax Publishers
Attention: Sales Department
15 West 26th Street
New York, NY 10010
212/685-6610   FAX 212/685-3916

Visit our website:
www.metrobooks.com

# ACKNOWLEDGMENTS

First and foremost, thanks to tractor collectors. These individuals and their families are keeping an important part of our heritage alive.
All across America, enthusiasts are spending their precious time and their children's inheritance on tractors. In many ways, their efforts are
more important than those of museums, because they are keeping tractors vital. Thank you all for your endowments. The kids will understand someday.
Second, my heartfelt thanks to the dozens of researchers and historians, both amateur and professional, who have created such an important archive of documentation about
tractors and the industry over the years. Scholars, such as C.H. Wendel and Lorry Dunning and dozens of others, have shared their information, benefiting all of us.
Third, my appreciation to all those enthusiasts who write a newsletter, maintain a database, or help put on a tractor show. A great deal of data about antique tractors is now
available on the Internet, helping tractor enthusiasts in all corners of the world to find those missing parts and gather information about their machines. It's a small fraternity
with a large heart. Those folks who help by putting on another pot of coffee for the committee planning the next tractor show should be appreciated, too, and I do.
And finally, my special thanks to my husband, Hans, and the other members of my personal cast and crew. Thanks for being there.

Till our tracks cross again,
*April Halberstadt*

*For Esther Hope and*
*Patrick Clark*

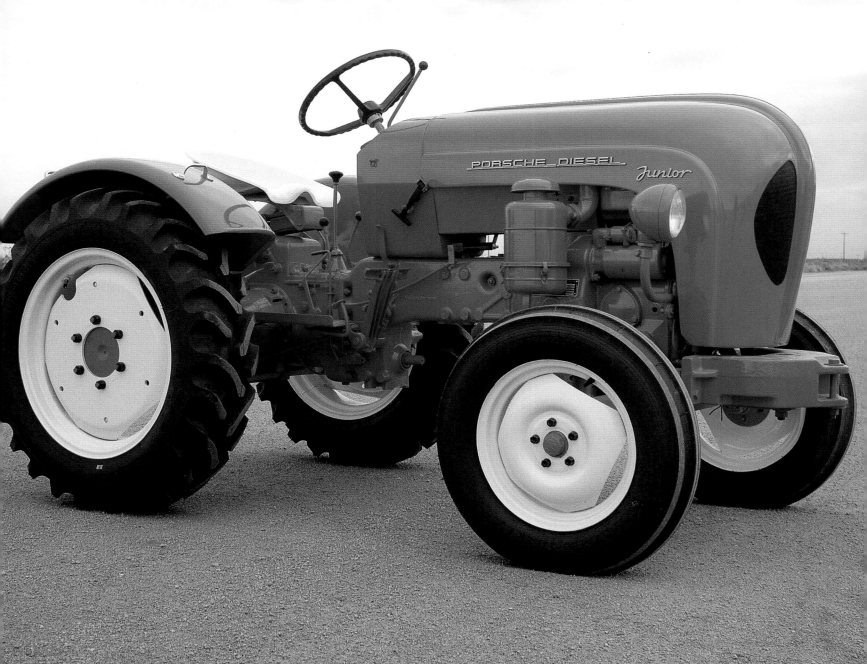

# CONTENTS

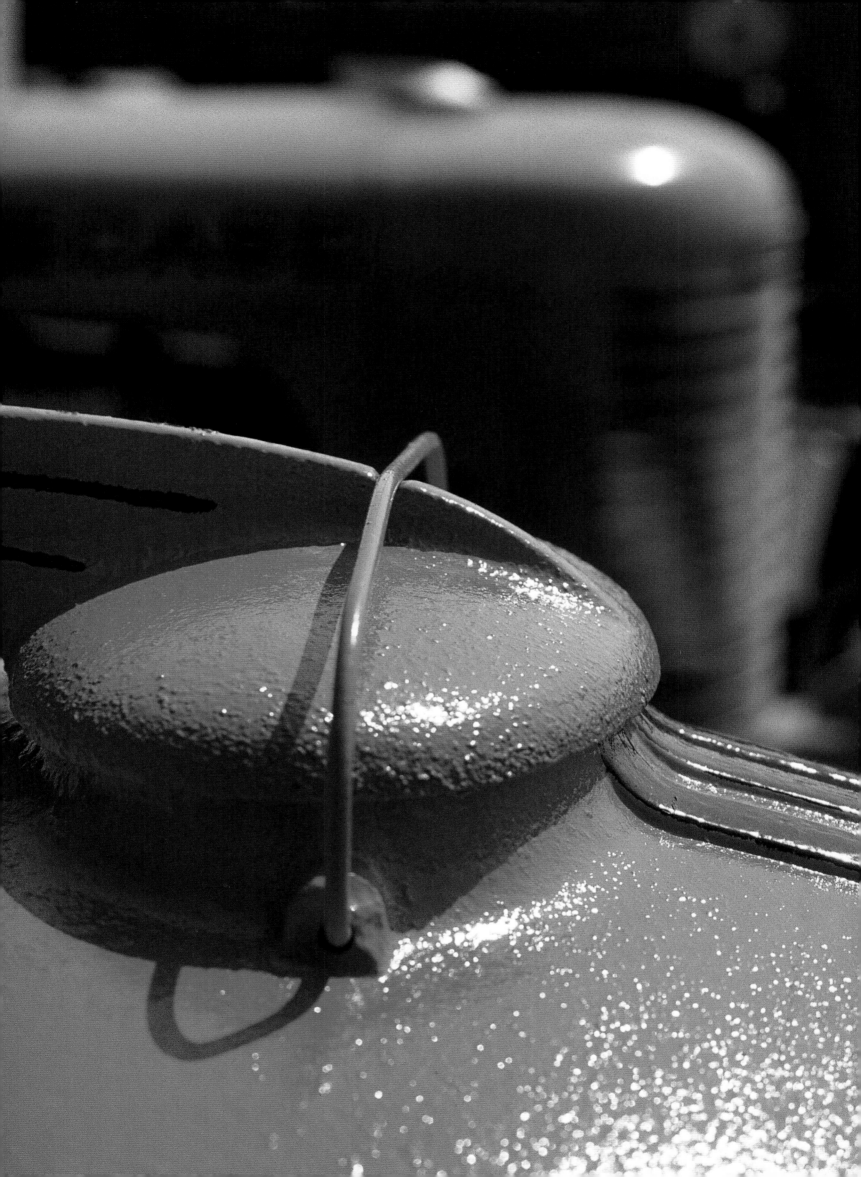

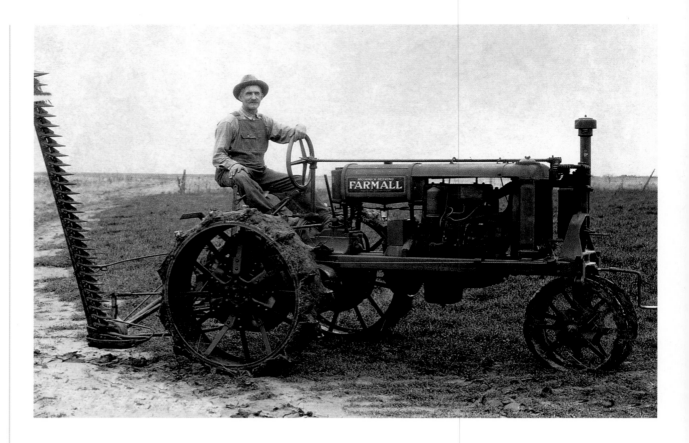

# INTRODUCTION

**W**hat is it about tractors that folks find so fascinating? Stray kittens, lost dogs, and abandoned tractors . . . our hearts go out to all of them. We look for any excuse to drag them home and love them. We give them names and treat them like members of the family. Some of these old tractors have been in the barn for more than thirty years. Why are we so reluctant to give them up?

Perhaps more than any other piece of machinery, tractors tell the story of America at the crossroads. A unique and totally American invention, the tractor brought a profound change to the economy, culture, and landscape of the United States and affected the entire world in the process. Introduced around the turn of the twentieth century, the tractor was a machine whose time had come, one that had been imagined for years by dreamers and tinkers alike. Countless amateur and professional mechanics—among them Henry Ford—dabbled with the tractor idea, putting little gasoline motors onto all sorts of wheeled frames in hopes of building that better mousetrap that would send farmers beating a path to their door.

Many critics and thinkers at the turn of the century bemoaned mechanization, noting that the human race was becoming enslaved by machines. But the tractor was something of a godsend when it

# BELLEVILLE THRESHING MACHINERY

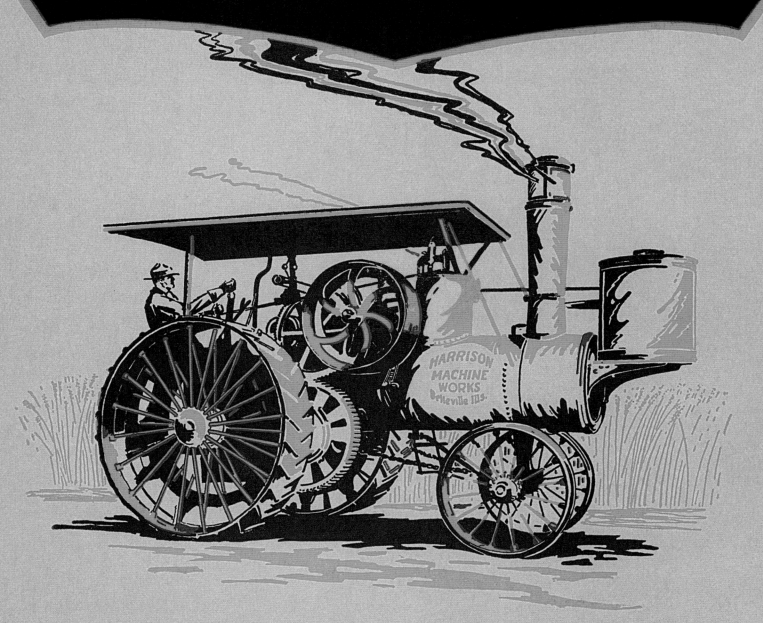

MANUFACTURED BY

## HARRISON MACHINE WORKS

### BELLEVILLE, ILLINOIS.

U·S·A·

first appeared just after 1900. The Homestead Act of the 1860s had given away land to any willing farmer, 160 acres per person (a married couple could claim 320 acres). Such huge tracts of land were far more than the average person or even couple could possibly cultivate on their own. Yet, suddenly, here was a machine that liberated the average farmer from a life of backbreaking labor and allowed him to become his own master. Now one farmer became capable of cultivating a substantial piece of land.

Finally, here was a piece of affordable machinery that would mean independence and prosperity for agricultural America. The tractor brought a new social order to the country, one that enabled each and every farmer to own and operate a personalized small business. It helped create a new economy and brought agriculture into the twentieth century, right alongside the titans of the Industrial Revolution.

Articles in popular journals frequently mourn the passing of what they refer to as "the family farm," but recent statistics show that eighty-five percent of American farms are still owned by families. While agribusiness holdings may be substantial, the small farmer still remains an important presence. Affordable tractors made that possible.

The 1990 U.S. Census showed that less than two percent of the American population considered themselves farmers. The American farm has become so efficient that this tiny percentage of the population now feeds the remaining ninety-eight percent, with food to spare. From the outset, tractors made farmers extraordinarily productive; in the years since their invention, every improvement and innovation on the tractor has improved the efficiency of the American farmer.

American agricultural technology has been a leader for a century, and tractors and other farm machinery have been the nation's contribution to our hungry world. J.I. Case was exporting machinery to Chile in 1885 and to many other South American countries by 1900. Case threshers and tractors first went to Russia in 1907 and International Harvester established its first European plant in Sweden in 1904. The Oliver Company's export of machinery to Europe in 1914 inadvertently brought tremendous financial hardship to Oliver when World War I interfered with payment.

*BELOW:* **Big Red, otherwise known as the International Harvester Company, soon captured the lead in the tractor marketplace with their introduction of the "Farmall." It remained a popular machine over the decades, living up to its name as an indispensable tool for the farmer. The model M was introduced in 1939 and remains a favorite today of both owners and collectors.**

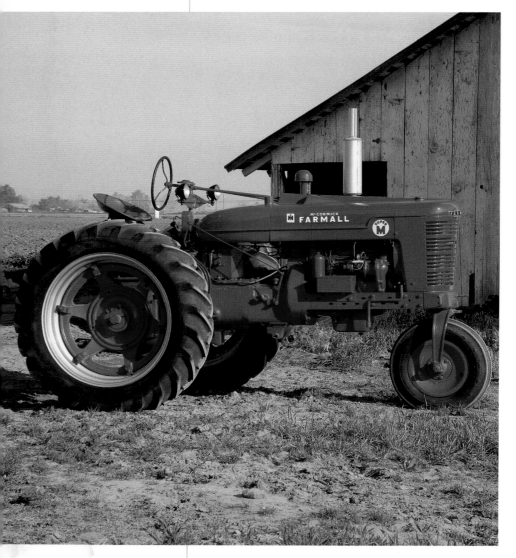

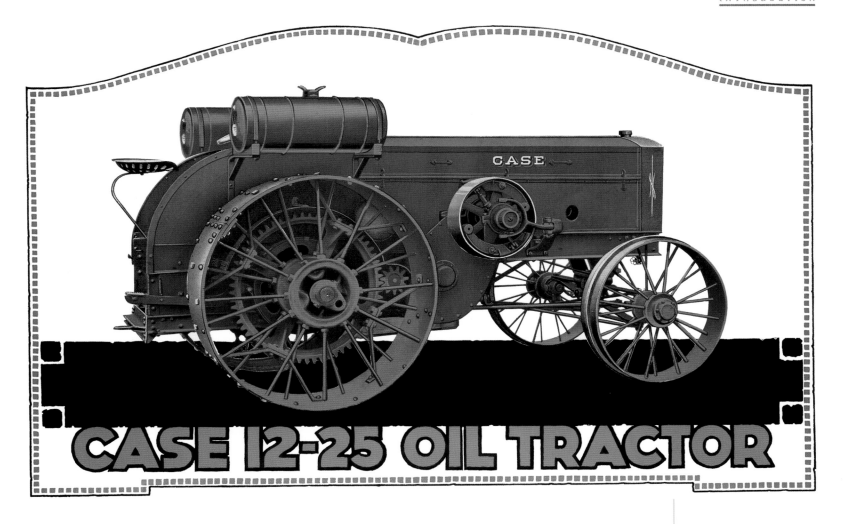

# CASE 12-25 OIL TRACTOR

*Power farming* was a concept introduced by Hart-Parr sales manager W. H. Williams, one of the industry's early super salesmen, to describe an entirely new way to farm. It was a new idea and described not simply the use of a tractor, but a different way of planning, harvesting, and marketing farm products. It was a slogan that quickly gained widespread use because it accurately described an agricultural revolution.

No longer entirely at the mercy of the weather, farmers now had tremendous flexibility. A tractor allowed the farmer to gather his crop quickly in case of impending storms and to plant or plow without depending on hired help. The average two-horse hitch might plow two furrows at a time; with a tractor, by contrast, the farmer could plant three or four, depending on the soil. In Williams's view, the tractor offered farmers deliverance from endless toil.

Why do we love tractors? Because there are such good stories associated with them—stories like the saga of tractor pioneers Hart and Parr, the inventors of the modern tractor; stories about Henry Ford and his "handshake agreement" with inventor Harry Ferguson; stories about Ford, the man who really wanted to build a tractor, not an automobile; and stories about competition and innovation, struggle and success, failure and heartbreak.

Every old tractor tells its own story. Perhaps that is one of the reasons that so many people are interested in the vintage tractor, the history of the factory that built it, and the history of the people who

*ABOVE: **Successful tractor builders, such as the J.I. Case Company, would be major corporations for more than a century.** BELOW: **Less fortunate designers, such as U.S. Tractor & Machinery Company, builder of the Uncle Sam, would disappear after just a few years.***

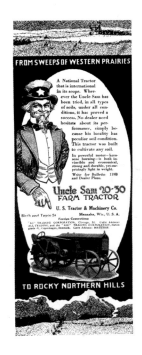

11

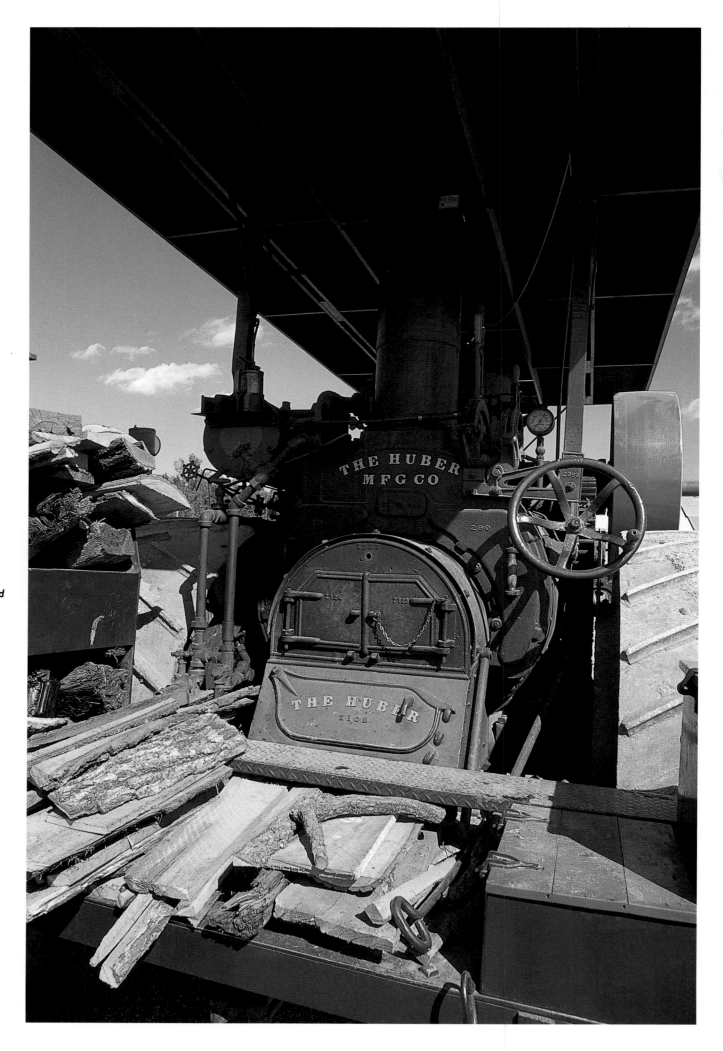

RIGHT: **Operating a steam tractor was hot, dirty, and dangerous work. The big machines required a crew of two or three skilled operators, not exactly a job that the average farmer was trained to manage. The firebox had to be fed with care to maintain constant heat in the boilers, and the steam pressure gauges had to be vigilantly monitored.**

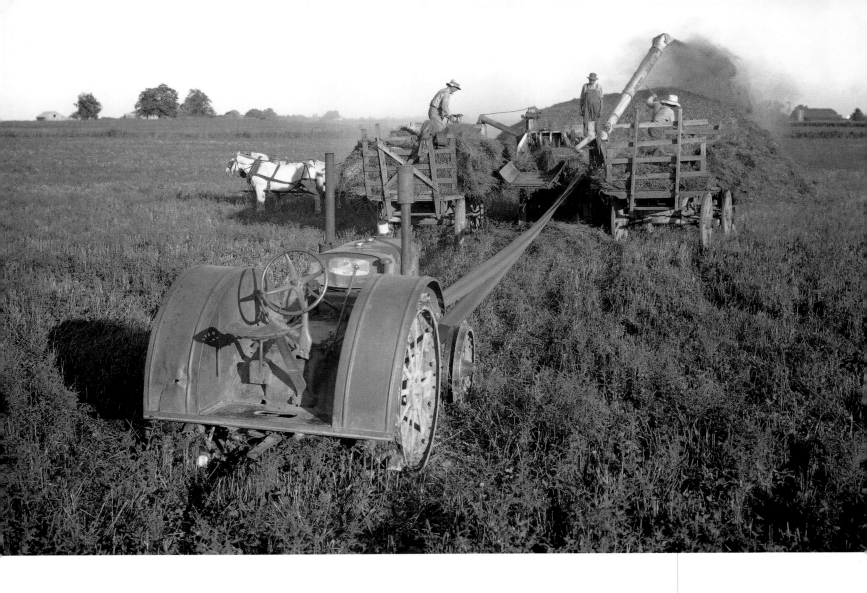

owned it. Many tractor collectors are farmers who still have Grandpa's tractor out in the shed, a beloved family heirloom.

Tractor names intrigue us; they are wonderful and colorful. The Bates "Steel Mule" from Joliet, Illinois, was a short-lived machine in the crawler family. It featured tracked rear wheels and a conventional front drive. Names like the Silver King, the Happy Farmer, and the Iron Horse identified machines of great promise. One important old favorite, now long gone, was called the Bull. Advertised as "the Bull with the Pull," it was the machine to beat in the early part of the twentieth century.

Old tractors have regional significance, too. Certain names stand out because they are associated with a unique time and place in rural America. The Square Turn tractor was built in Norfolk, Nebraska, and the Samson Sieve Grip was made in Stockton, California. At one time, tractor builders were the biggest business in scores of American towns like Charles City, Iowa, or St. Charles, Missouri. Many collectors have a hometown favorite.

Certain agricultural areas of the Ohio Valley and the Midwest, especially Iowa and the Quad Cities area, seem to have the greatest numbers of tractor makers, but there are rare and exotic tractors from all corners of farming America. Two of the rarest tractors, the Bean Track-Pull and the Fageol (pronounced *FAD-jil*) were both designed for the orchards and vineyards of California. The Dill Harvesting Tractor was built in Little Rock, Arkansas, specifically for use in wet and swampy rice fields.

*ABOVE:* **Replacing the steam tractor, a small but powerful gas tractor could deliver all the horsepower needed to operate this stationary thresher. When belted to another piece of farm equipment, the gasoline tractor became a portable power source that gave the farmer tremendous flexibility in the field.**

Tractor-building history provides us with clear lessons about the result of intense competition and market saturation. Dozens of tractor builders came and went in the years between 1910 and 1930. In just twenty short years, the number of tractor manufacturers soared to a height of 166 in 1920, then plummeted to only forty-seven by 1930. The Depression years cut even further into the numbers of tractor builders. Today only two major builders remain, John Deere and Case IH.

*BELOW: Reliability was extremely important to the consumer. The tractor became the farmer's most essential tool, allowing him to become an independent businessman.*

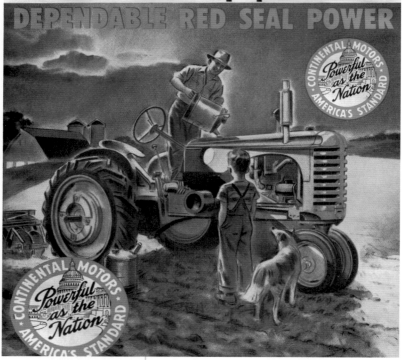

Why do we love tractors? Because they are the first machines that many Americans of a certain generation learned to drive. Because they sound good. Because they were the country's first RV, an all-terrain vehicle that put the driver in the open air, showing him all the sights. Because they remind us of our dads . . . or our grandfathers. Because they symbolize the independent way of life.

So this little book is a quick overview of some of our favorite tractors. It doesn't try to cover all the unique and important machines. But hopefully a few favorites are here, along with some of the history about what makes them so special and so wonderful. I think tractors are special, and I hope you do, too.

*RIGHT: Cold and lonely, abandoned and unwanted, discarded machines such as this tractor pull at our heart strings. We can be comforted by remembering that one man's trash is another's treasure.*

*OPPOSITE: The Golden Age of tractors came to a close with machines like the International Harvester 560, introduced in the late 1950s. The boxy styling is not as appealing as earlier models.*

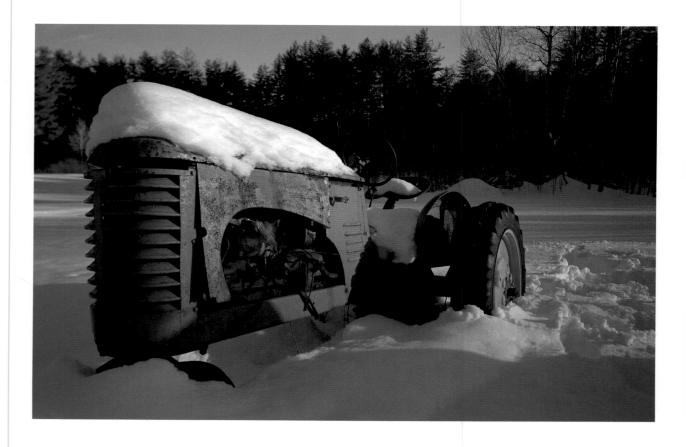

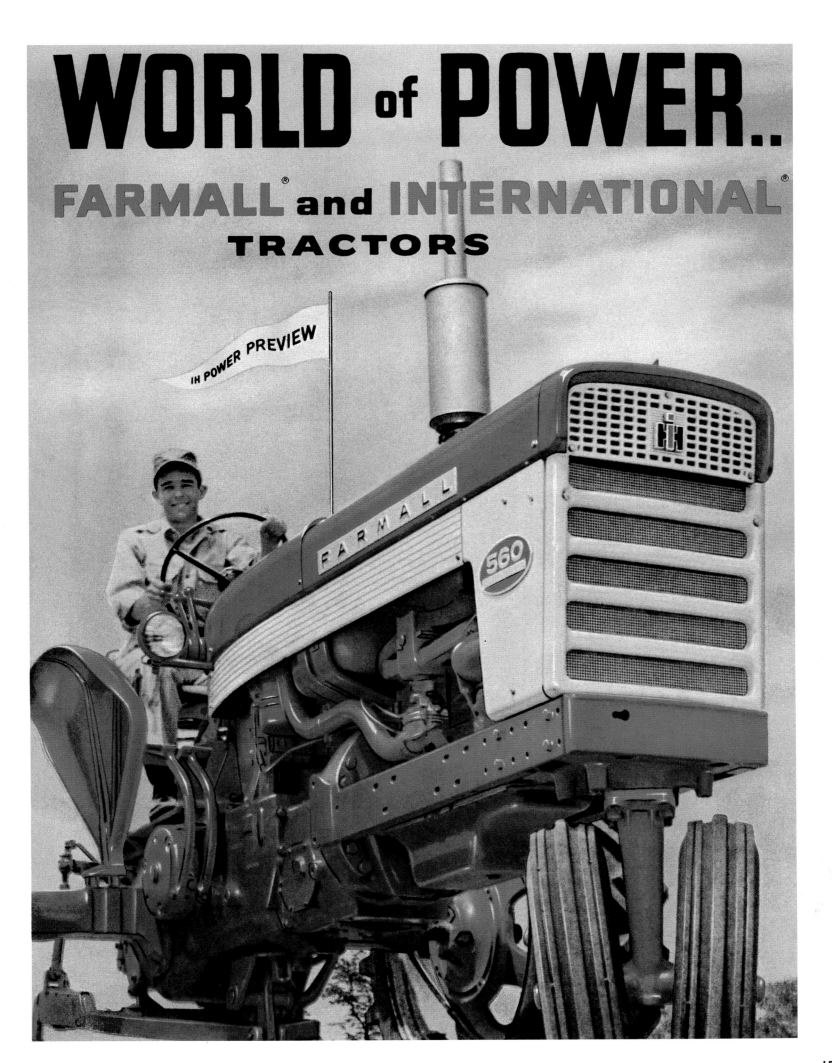

# WORLD of POWER..
## FARMALL® and INTERNATIONAL®
### TRACTORS

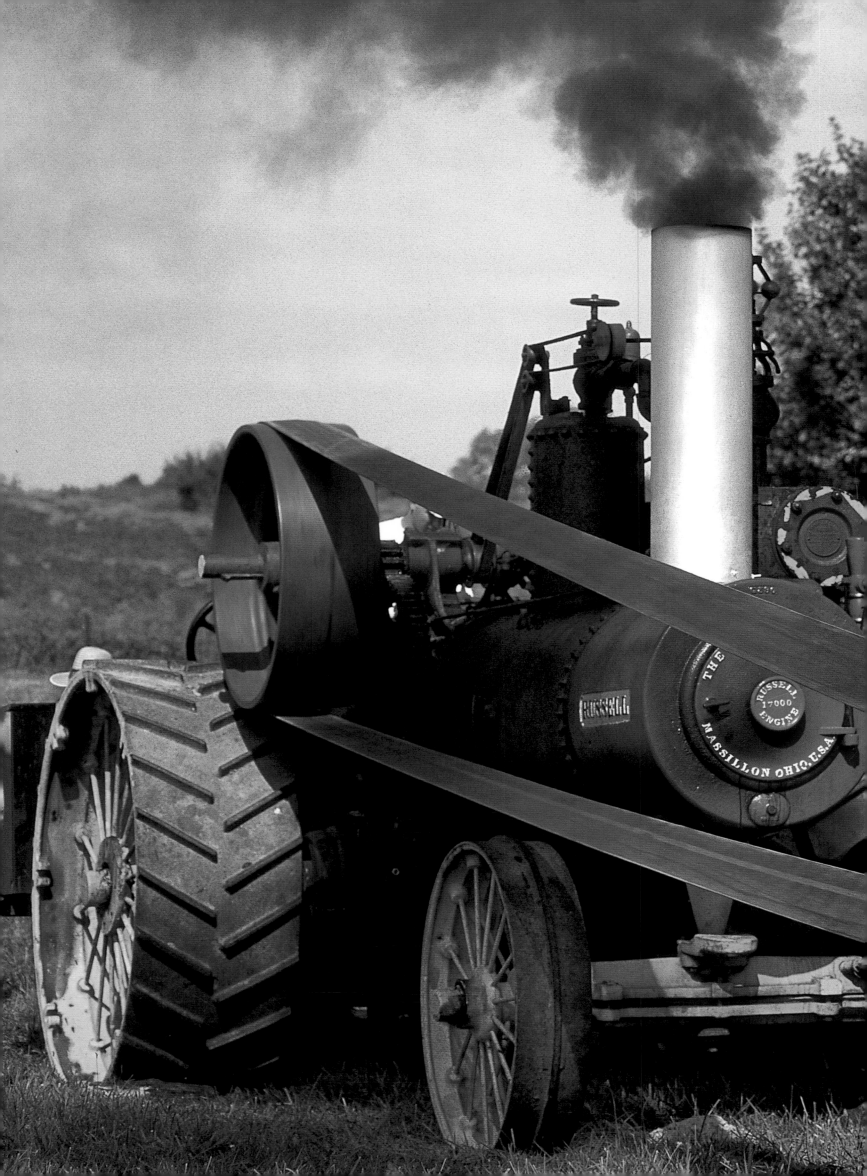

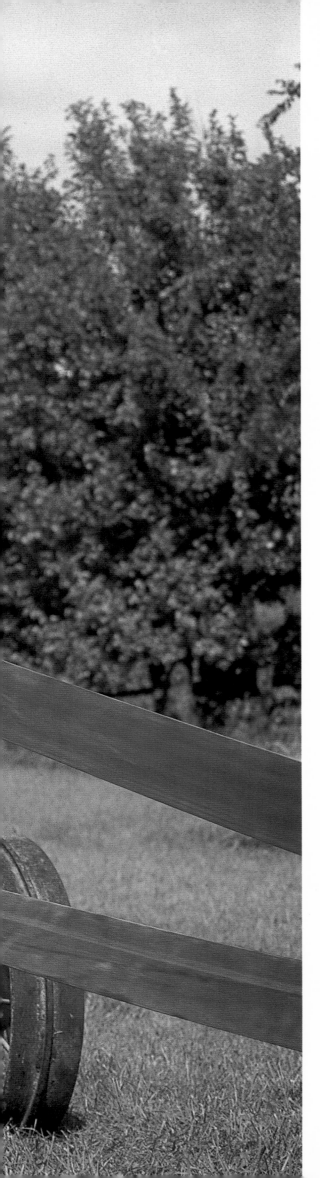

# THE GOOD OLD DAYS

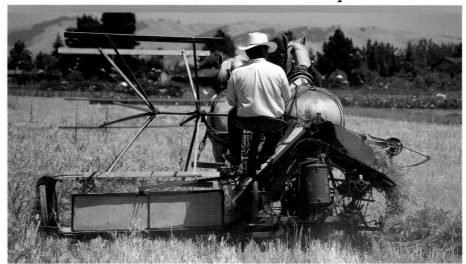

## Chapter One

In the good old days of farming, back around 1900, there were two kinds of horsepower. The first was supplied by Dobbin or the Old Gray Mare, the second by that great technology of the nineteenth century, the steam engine. The farmers of the upper Great Plains, the breadbasket of America, used steam tractors to plow, plant, and harvest their crops. In general, the rest of the farmers, those in the South and West, used horses.

At the turn of the twentieth century, well-to-do farmers already owned all sorts of ingenious machinery that helped them plow and plant, cut and harvest their crops. American ingenuity had developed the mechanized reaper, the combined harvester, and an entire range of plows designed for every type of soil condition. Mechanized seeders and weeders of all sorts first arrived on American farms after the Civil War and reached a high level of refinement by the end of the century. Power for this machinery was first supplied by horses or, occasionally, by mules.

LEFT: *The steam traction machine was an extremely powerful alternative to horses, but much too expensive to own and difficult for the average farmer to operate.*

ABOVE: *Pulled by horses, this reaper was just one of the marvelous labor-saving machines that Yankee ingenuity had devised decades before tractors appeared.*

## Horses and Draft Agriculture

When we talk about the good old days in farming, we have to mention horses. As popular as tractors and mechanized farming later became, many farmers were reluctant to part with a system of farming that they had grown up with. In many parts of America, petroleum fuels for tractors were not readily available until well after World War II. Horses were a lot easier, and cheaper, to maintain. Horse farming—that is, farming using horses—remains all across America, and is undergoing a resurgence in popularity.

These days, farmers are increasingly using horses to plow and plant, particularly farmers who keep draft animals. Bred to work, these large animals need meaningful chores to perform in order to train well. There are several reasons why some farmers use draft horses. Some feel it is a good environmental practice. Some like the intellectual challenge of training and managing a team. Some are concerned about the disappearance of draft animals and enjoy maintaining the domestic breeds.

There are only a handful of heavy draft breeds: Clydesdales and Percherons, Belgians and Shires, and the affectionate Suffolks. These types of horses were used for the heaviest farm work, such as pulling multiple plows or hauling the thresher into the field for the annual harvest. Far more common on the average farm were cross-breeds, smaller horses that could be used to pull a single plow or take a cart to market.

Of course, for some farmers, horse farming has always been a way of life. The Old Order Amish, eschewing machinery and modern convenience, have continued to depend on horses in their daily farm life. Despite the constraints of this horse-powered way of life, the number of Amish families is growing as more and more people are finding the simple life and quiet pace of Amish life increasingly attractive.

While it had been essential to have a good working horse on the farm, farmers quickly recognized the advantages of mechanized agriculture even before tractors actually arrived on the scene. It was not difficult to weigh the costs of feeding and housing a horse against the costs of operating a tractor. Horses eat every day, working or not, and require constant attention. But a tractor could sit neglected in the barn for weeks at a time without harm; it cost nothing to own a tractor during the winter months when it wasn't in use. And while many farmers hung on to their beloved horses, declaring that no machine could offer the kind of loyalty and affection a horse provided, most of them joined the

BELOW: *Farming with horses remains popular in many parts of America, especially in the Amish communities. A matched pair of Belgian draft horses pulls a hay wagon, just as they have done for centuries.*

OPPOSITE: *Plowing is hard work for the horse and for the farmer. Walking in soft soil with dust filling your boots and your lungs is a nasty chore. Even with a good pair of horses it requires considerable strength and practice to manage both the team and a plow.*

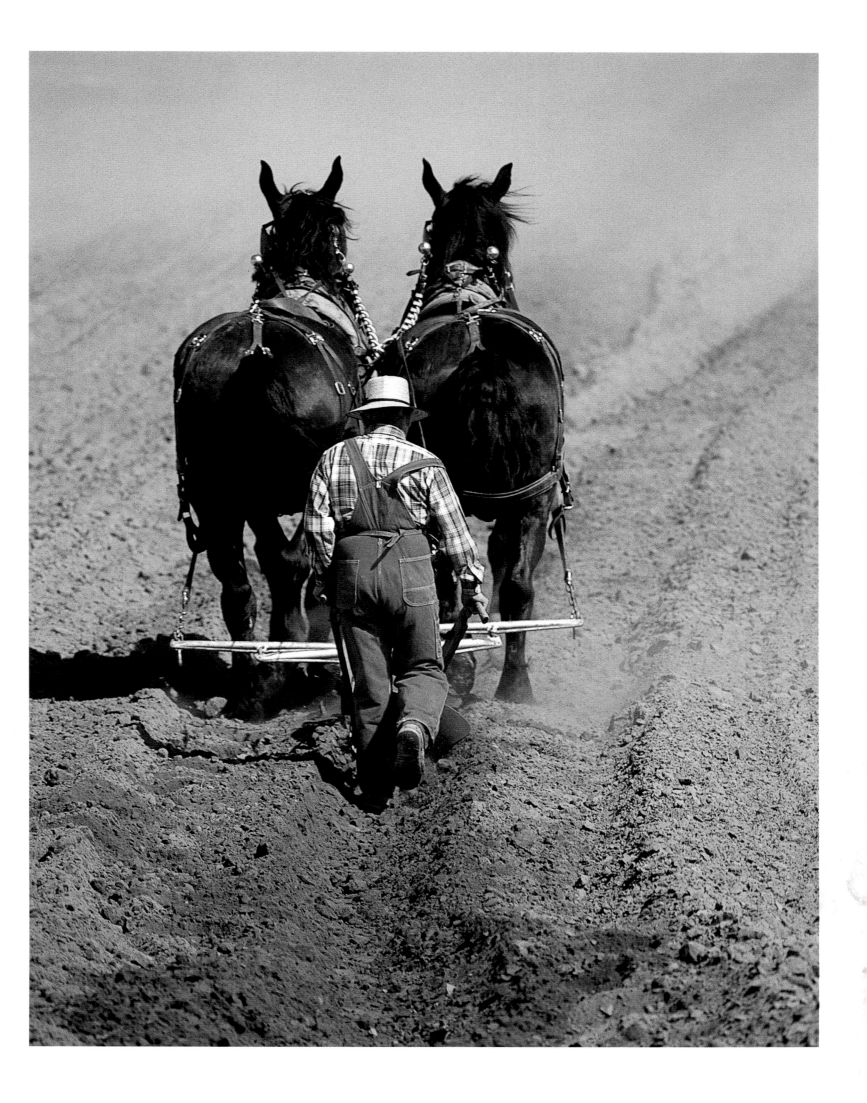

agricultural revolution as quickly as they could. And even if they couldn't get a nuzzle from their tractors, they still developed bonds with their machines similar to those they had once (and perhaps still) shared with their cherished work horse.

Tractors were an idea whose time had come. And although some farmers continued to rely on their horses—one source estimates that there were seventeen million horses still performing agricultural work at the end of World War II—chugging over the hill was the technology that would help create the new and prosperous America.

## Steaming Up: The First Tractors

By the 1880s, the steam traction engine appeared on the scene, developed by agricultural equipment pioneer J.I. Case. Although steam power had been an important power source in America for decades

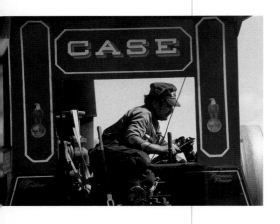

*BELOW: **Steam tractor operators need special training in order to maintain and operate the boilers. They are a vanishing breed, though a few young men still seem willing to learn this dangerous trade.***

(powering boats and locomotives since the 1830s), it was not practical or affordable for small-scale operations like farming or construction. Steam boilers were dangerous contraptions that frequently blew up, often with spectacular and catastrophic consequences.

Jerome Increase Case, a builder of agricultural machinery, designed and built his first thresher in 1842. He frequently went to the field to demonstrate its operation, and he sold it and serviced it; in fact, it was not uncommon for an unhappy customer to find that the mechanic repairing his balky thresher was J.I. Case himself. More than just a builder of

*RIGHT: **Not for sissies, the driver's seat of a steam engine is a thrilling place to sit. The sensation can be overwhelming; the smell, the sound and the pulse of a steamer under full power is incredible. No wonder steam engineers are still regarded with awe and respect.***

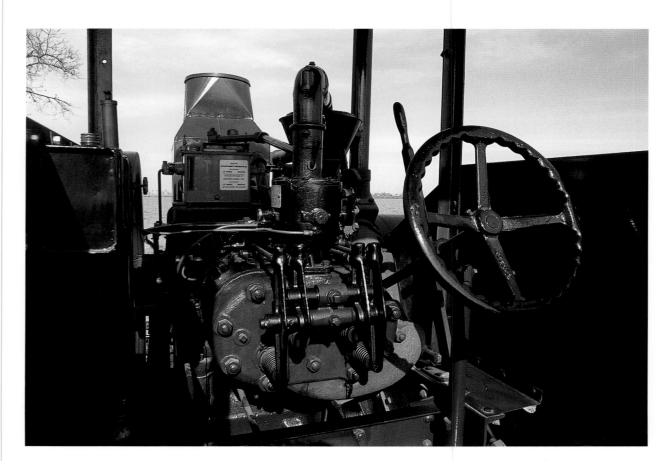

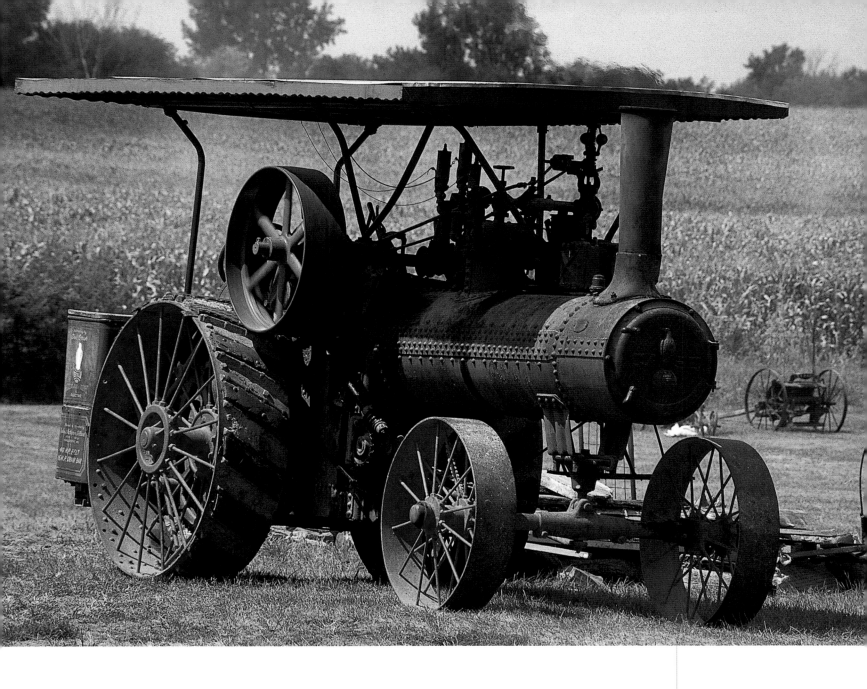

threshers, Case also developed a line of related agricultural equipment, and he was always looking for ways to improve farm production.

Case is credited with introducing the first practical steam engine to the farmer. He brought it out a few years after the Civil War, building seventy-five steam engines for farm use in 1870. The huge contraption was hauled into the field by horses and was then harnessed to the belts and pulleys that drove the threshers. Large and clumsy though it was, the machine proved useful and efficient for the large wheat farming operations in the upper Great Plains, across the Dakotas, and in the expanses of Canada—farms that covered thousands of acres.

Operating a steam engine was a major undertaking, requiring a trained boiler engineer and a fireman in addition to a supporting cast of fuel wagons and a water tank to keep it in operation. Finally, it required tremendous caution to operate, since flying ash from the smokestack might easily set an entire grain field afire.

By 1878, Case had designed a machine that could roll onto the field under its own steam. The next giant technological leap was a self-propelled machine with steering, operated by a two-man crew of

*ABOVE: Jerome Increase Case developed and refined the steam traction engine, introducing his first machine in 1876. It is estimated that the Case company built nearly 36,000 machines during the fifty years of steamer production. Surprisingly, the greatest numbers of Case steam machines were built between 1900 and 1915, after gas tractors had already appeared.*

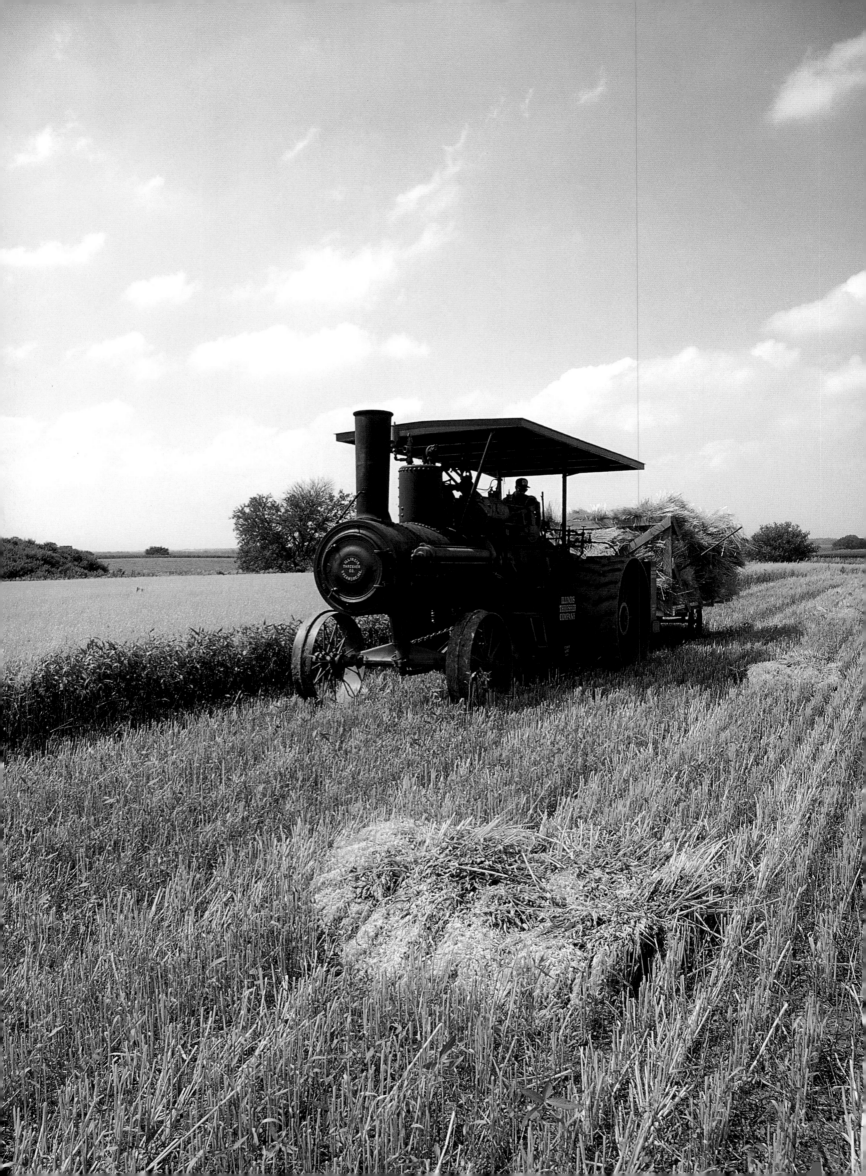

boiler tender and operator. The machine was now becoming known as a *steam traction engine*—an engine that not only could provide its own motive power but could pull another piece of equipment as well.

Steam tractors rapidly became lighter, stronger, and more maneuverable. Very soon, the J.I. Case Company had a lot of competition from many other builders. Steam engines for farmers were the major offering of the Avery Company, founded in 1877 in Galesburg, Illinois, and later relocated to Peoria. The Advance-Rumely traction engine first appeared in 1888 in Battle Creek, Michigan, and that firm built steamers until 1928. Aultman & Taylor, a builder located in Mansfield, Ohio, is credited with turning out nearly six thousand engines before closing its doors in 1924.

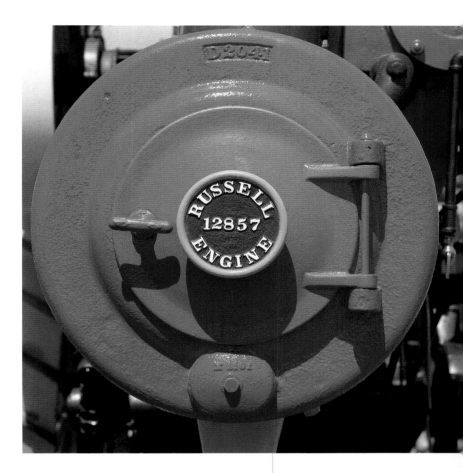

Steamers were a proven technology, and there were plenty of folks who knew how to operate them. A steamer could plow five acres in an hour and in an average day could do fifty times as much work as a single plowman with his two-horse hitch. By 1900, an esti- mated five thousand steam engines were being built each year, most of them by a handful of companies including Case, Huber, Advance-Rumely, Aultman & Taylor, and several smaller concerns such as Keck-Gonnerman in Mt. Vernon, Indiana, and the innovative Best Manufacturing Company in San Leandro, California. Best would build some of the largest steamers ever seen.

Steam tractor building was over by 1930; the Great Depression finally closed the doors on the last of the manufacturers. Thousands of steam tractors were already in service on American farms, though, so steamers continued to perform in widespread operations until mid-century, and were especially important during the years of World War II, when petroleum fuels were hard to find. Since steamers can operate on almost any kind of combustible—wood, hay, even old corncobs—they proved to be a valuable and highly adaptable piece of machinery during the Depression and later in wartime.

Steam traction engines paved the way for the farm tractor. Nearly as soon as the steam engine appeared, inventors began thinking of ways to make it smaller and lighter. Many inventors tried the approach of bolting a gasoline engine onto the frame of a steamer. Not surprisingly, the first tractors looked like steamers.

Farming with steam is gone now, replaced by gasoline-powered tractors that are just as powerful and a lot safer. Steam power depends on pressure from a boiler and boiler tenders have faded from the scene.

*ABOVE:* **The Russell Company was a major builder of steam tractors. This is the faceplate of the 1906 Russell owned and restored by collector Glen Christoffersen. Operating tractors such as this beauti- fully restored machine are frequently a fea- tured attraction at farm shows and fairs during the summer.**

*OPPOSITE:* **One of the great virtues of the steam traction machine was its tremendous power and its ability to work in weather that was too hot for horses. For these reasons, steam trac- tors, like this offering from the Illinois Thresher Company, were quickly adapted for use in both con- struction and road building projects.**

# PAT ERTEL: MR. TRACTOR

PAT ERTEL recently took delivery on a new drawbar for his 1935 Silver King, but he hasn't had time to install it. He has been too busy, finishing up a couple of books in addition to handling his regular job as editor of *Antique Power* magazine.

Pat is frequently singled out as the driving force behind the current enthusiasm for tractor collection and restoration. Mild-mannered and intellectual, his quiet personality seems at odds with the demeanor of the average tractor enthusiast, but then Clark Kent was a good cover for Superman.

*Antique Power* magazine came to life in November of 1988, and it was an idea whose time had come. Today the magazine inspires hundreds of tractor enthusiasts who no longer hide their hobby in garages and barns. Pat reports that the interest in tractors is still growing—much faster than he could ever have imagined.

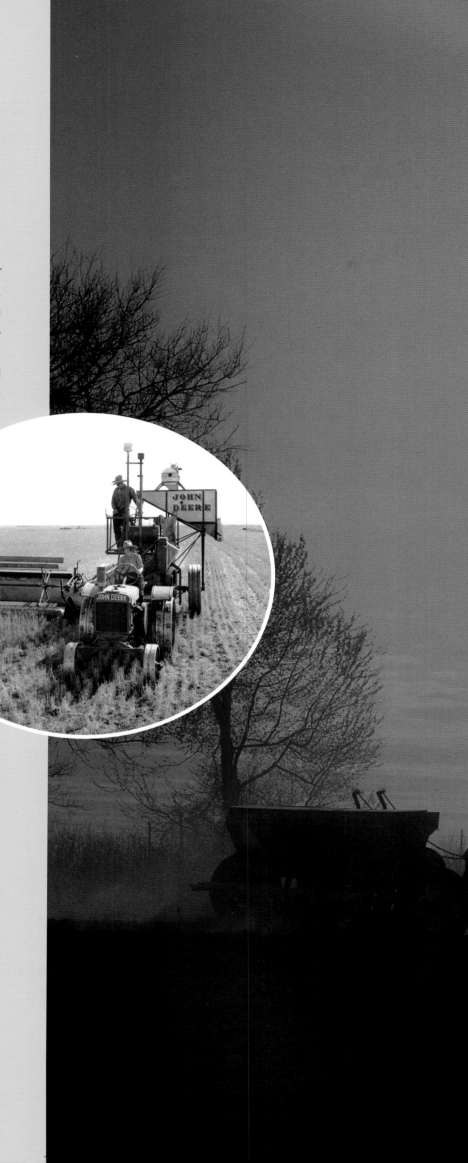

Pat Ertel is a materials engineer by training and by trade, and a technology enthusiast by inclination. For years, his day job was at Wright-Patterson Air Force Base near Dayton, Ohio, and most of his evenings were spent in class, keeping up with aerospace technology. In the fall of 1988 he was burned out and decided to take some time off. But after about a month of lying on the floor, watching TV, and drinking beer, he realized that he was bored.

One magic day he saw a restored Emerson-Brantingham tractor on a flatbed trailer, being hauled to who knows where. He followed it in order to take a closer look at this rare vintage tractor and found himself at an antique tractor show being held at Hewston Woods Park. The clouds parted, the sun shone, and the hidden kingdom of antique tractors was revealed to Pat.

Pat recalls that when he went to the tractor show, memories came flooding back. There were memories of the John Deere Model B from his youth and the first tractor he had learned to drive, the family's Ford 9N. He wanted to learn more about tractors and subscribed to *Gas Engine*

magazine. But that magazine did not satisfy his curiosity about the history of tractor technology.

For some time, Pat had been writing and taking pictures for a Porsche newsletter called the 356 Registry. When he complained to a friend about the need for a good publication about old tractors, his friend observed, "Sounds like an opportunity to me." So *Antique Power* appeared in 1988 as a spare-time hobby and a substitute for evening classes.

Within two years, Pat was making more money with his magazine and having lots more fun with tractors than with aerospace engineering. He continued to run *Antique Power* out of his garage until 1995 when he outgrew his space. In 1997, the publication office was moved to Yellow Springs, Ohio, a town it still calls home.

Pat now owns four tractors, all chunks of personal nostalgia. He bought his first "new" tractor in 1992, a Ford 9N just like the one he had learned to drive at age nine. He bought a replacement for his boyhood John Deere Model B and reluctantly sold it last year when the original owner appeared. The buyer had spent years tracking down this machine from his youth, so what else could a sentimental softy like Pat do? He just had to sell it. Tractors have hearts and souls, too.

The Model B has been replaced with a 1930 Deere GP, which Pat describes as a "serious project." It keeps company with a machine that falls into the classification of a Lesser Known Classic, a 1935 Silver King. Bringing up the rear is a tiny Sears garden tractor from the early 1950s. It's another nostalgia tractor for Pat, a reminder of childhood times reading the Sears catalog and looking longingly at a "real" tractor, one scaled to just the right size for a small boy.

*Antique Power* magazine is the handbook for hundreds of tractor enthusiasts, newcomers, and old-timers alike. This periodical provides inspiration, advice, and good, solid information about tractors of all ages. Thanks, Pat, for first following that old Emerson-Brantingham down your own Yellow Brick Road.

INSET: *An affordable tractor manufacturer like John Deere allowed the average farmer to manage large acreage without outside help, creating a new economic order for America.*

LEFT: *Owning and operating a vintage tractor is a hobby that has been growing rapidly, thanks to its many enthusiasts.*

Steam traction engines never suited the average farmer anyway; they always required the attention of an experienced operator. And one other drawback: they were enormously heavy. Many a rural bridge collapsed under the weight of a steamer on its way to a nearby farm.

Today many of those old steamers have taken on new life as collectors' items. These antiques require a good deal of care, but serious collectors drive thousands of miles to demonstrate and show their steam engines. Transporting steamers is not easy; they must travel on trailers hauled by semis. Owning and showing a vintage steamer takes an enormous amount of dedication and knowledge—plus a fat pocketbook.

One of the most awe-inspiring events for steam tractor enthusiasts and owners takes place every year in Rollag, Minnesota, up near the Canadian border. Hundreds of steam tractors gather for a demonstration and show. Seeing and hearing all these enormous machines rumbling and clanking at once makes for a very dramatic event. The sky turns black with the smoke from hundreds of engines. The event is an extraordinary tribute to the thousands of steam fans who keep the technology alive.

*BELOW: Tractor shows have been an important marketing strategy since before the turn of the twentieth century. The annual fair was a good place for the local farmer to compare the benefits of various machines and keep informed of new models and innovations.*

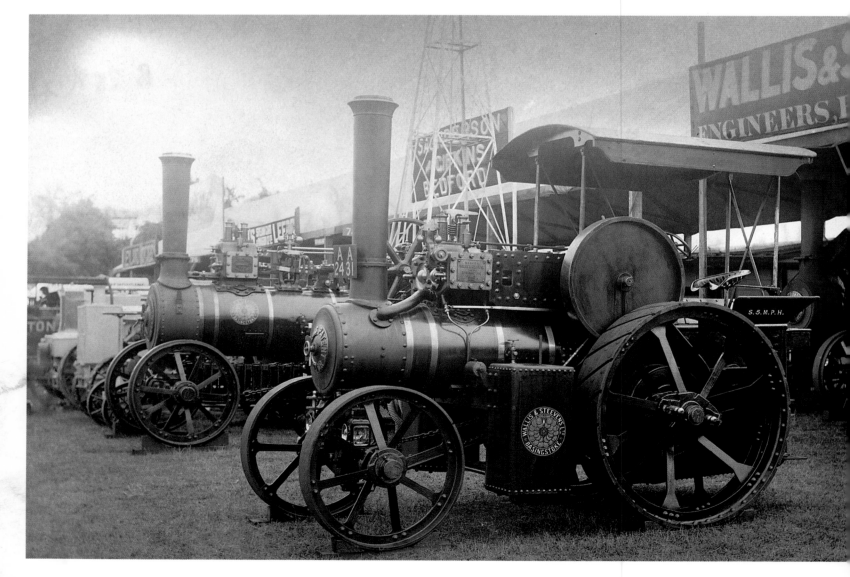

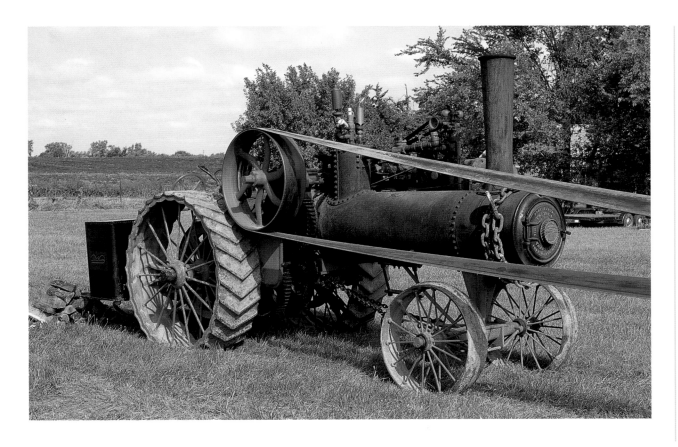

## Real Horsepower

Tractors were built to replace horses. In order to assess a tractor's capability in the field, early tractors were rated by horsepower. How much pull is one horsepower? One old farm handbook tells us that it is the amount of power required to lift thirty-three thousand pounds one foot in one minute, or the equivalent. And that is the effort that the average horse is able to demonstrate. In the old days, tractor horsepower was measured at the tractor flywheel by a device known as a Prony brake. Used for the old steam tractors, this instrument was adapted to evaluate the kerosene and gasoline tractors.

Tractors were historically used for two different chores. The first was simply as a power source: the tractor was parked in the field and belted up to a threshing machine or another piece of farm equipment. The second chore placed a much heavier load on the tractor's engine. Pulling a plow required an engine to provide enough muscle to drive the tractor, pull a heavy piece of equipment, and overcome the friction and drag of a field of sticky soil. Generally, the horsepower generated while plowing was about half of the resting load.

Because of the vastly different nature of these two jobs, tractors were usually given two horsepower numbers. Frequently these numbers were used in the model name. The Hart-Parr tractor, introduced in 1911, for example, had an engine rated at 30-horsepower while pulling a plow and 60-horsepower while resting. It was sold as the Hart-Parr 30-60, otherwise known as Old Reliable.

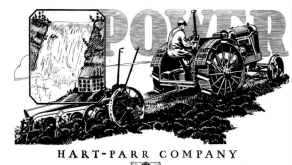

HART-PARR COMPANY

CHARLES CITY , IOWA
FOUNDERS OF THE TRACTOR INDUSTRY

*ABOVE:* **Power farming became a marketing slogan for the Hart-Parr Company, the folks who built the first marketable gasoline tractors. The concept quickly caught on.**

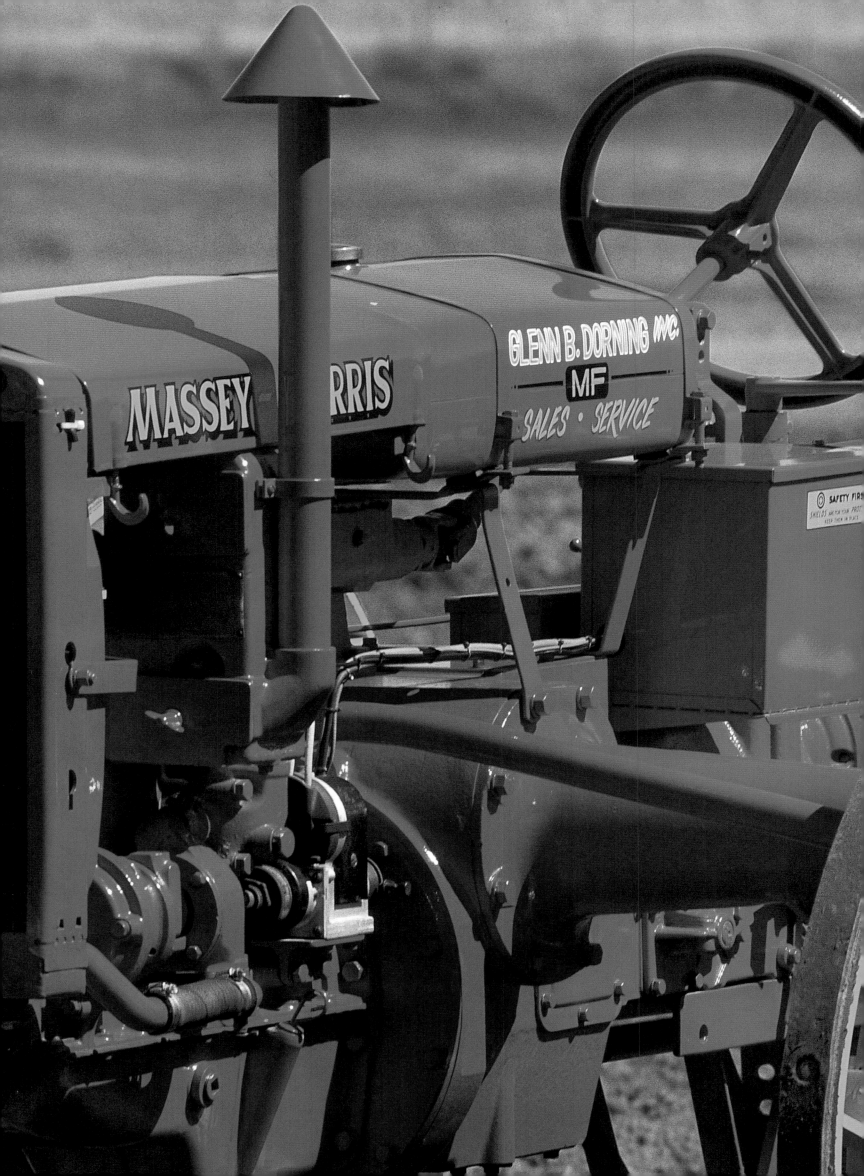

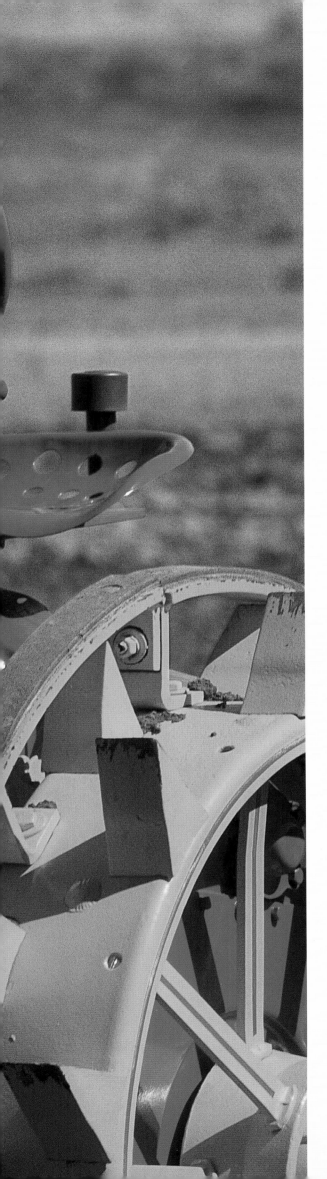

# TRACTORS GET GOING

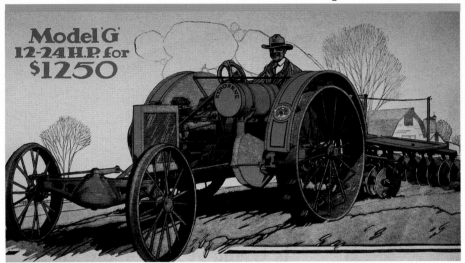

## Chapter Two

Model 'G'
12-24 H.P. for
$1250

**A**s a rule, farmers are conservatives. Some think of farmers, especially Old World farmers, as traditionalists. Unwilling to change, they stick with the tried and true. But agricultural historian Robert C. Williams points out that American farmers provide a marked contrast, noting that "in America, change is traditional." In addition, Americans have a long tradition of what has come to be known as Yankee ingenuity, priding themselves on their ideas and ability to make something better, faster, cheaper. So once the first tractor, the Hart-Parr, appeared in the field, dozens of mechanically inclined farmers were inspired to imitate and innovate on their own. Many of the most important developments in agricultural mechanization have come from the shops and workbenches of farmers. And what innovations were not achieved out in the barn were accomplished in the factory, as established agricultural manufacturers—like John Deere and International Harvester and automaker Henry Ford—got into the tractor game.

*ABOVE: A favorite with vintage tractor collectors, the Happy Farmer is now remembered as a machine that did not keep their owners happy for long.*

*LEFT: Collectors lavish a great deal of care and attention to detail on their prized vintage tractors. This glittering Massey-Harris is a simply stunning restoration.*

## The Tractor Is Born: The Hart-Parr

Since several enormous agricultural equipment builders already existed in America, most farmers who thought about it expected new machinery to be introduced by one of these giants, the firms with household names like Cyrus McCormick, William Deering, or J.I. Case. All these companies had stayed competitive through the years by buying innovation, taking over smaller firms that had a new machine to offer. And all these companies had deep pockets as well as large networks of distributors and salesmen.

Yet the gasoline tractor owes more of its heritage to automobile manufacturers than to traditional farm machinery builders. The development of the farm tractor actually began not in the laboratory of the J.I. Case Company, but with a couple of students in the little college town of Madison, Wisconsin.

Way back in 1894, an intense young man was standing in line at the University of Wisconsin admissions office. Charles Hart was from Charles City, Iowa, the son of a prosperous farmer. He started college in his home state but transferred from the famous agricultural school in Ames, Iowa, because he was interested in petroleum engineering and gasoline engines, and had heard that the school in Madison had a better program. As fate would have it, Hart struck up a conversation with another fellow in line, Charles Parr, a quiet and very serious student who was a few years older. Parr was also fascinated with gasoline engines and had also come to the University of Wisconsin because of its outstanding reputation. The two men decided to room together, a historic moment in tractor history.

BELOW: *One of the earliest "tricycle" tractors was developed by Case to compete with the wildly successful "Bull" tractor. The Case had a four cylinder engine and sold from 1915 to 1918, proving to be poorly maneuverable. But it was a direct response to both competition and the marketplace, forces that had begun to shape tractor design.*

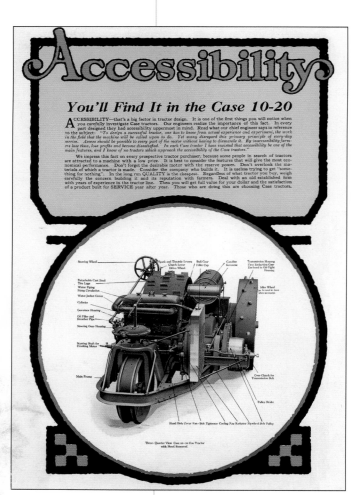

The meeting was provident, and the partnership would prove to be very productive. The two students would design, build, and sell gasoline engines before they even graduated from college. Recognizing their extraordinary talent, the university allowed the pair to use the university shops to build their engines. With this encouragement, the two young men set up a factory near the campus in order to manufacture gasoline power plants. Faculty members and other local investors supported their efforts, and the first Hart-Parr Company was officially incorporated in 1897.

The young inventors soon found themselves at odds with their more traditional investors. Hart and Parr were building and selling gasoline-powered stationary power plants, engines that would drive printing presses, pumps, and all sorts of other industrial machinery. Their little manufacturing business was very profitable. But the young inventors were interested in coming up with new products, most especially the development of a small gas-powered traction machine. They wanted to leave the business of building stationary plants and move on to greater challenges.

On a visit to his home in Iowa, Charles Hart complained to his father about his dilemma. His father suggested that Charles talk to a long-time family friend, a local banker named Charles Ellis. The banker offered Hart fifty thousand dollars to relocate his business, and by 1900 the entire operation moved and a new business was incorporated in Iowa. Charles Hart and Charles Parr, encouraged by banker Charles Ellis, established their new business in Charles City.

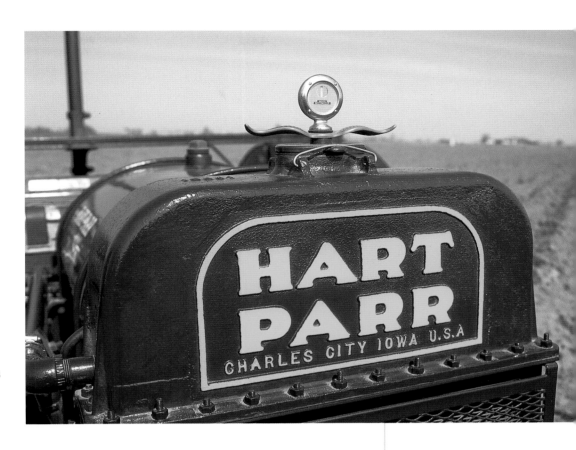

*ABOVE:* **Charles Hart and Charles Parr are credited with developing the first gasoline powered tractor. The exquisite detailing on this 1927 Hart-Parr is evidence of the stylistic enhancements that followed.**

Building on Hart and Parr's previous success, the new firm had a workable prototype by 1901 and delivered its first gasoline-powered tractor to a customer in 1902. Incidentally, in addition to developing the gasoline-powered tractor, the Hart-Parr firm was also pioneering new manufacturing methods. The engineering department at the University of Wisconsin had been a leader in developing the production techniques that we now know as assembly lines. Assembly line production would play a critical role in the success of automaker Henry Ford and other early automakers.

Assembly line production methods would be a key component in the success of the Hart-Parr operation. During the 1890s, the first Hart-Parr plant in Wisconsin had experimented with a modern assembly line, which included manufacturing and milling several subassemblies before final assembly. Small batches of parts were machined to maximize profitability and quality control. Meticulous shop notes were kept on procedures and tolerances for each batch. The new Charles City plant was specifically designed with these new manufacturing practices in mind.

Both of the first two early Hart-Parr engines were 30-horsepower tractors. The frames differed slightly but both traction machines reportedly functioned well. The first person to buy a gasoline-powered tractor was David Jennings of Clear Lake, Iowa. The second customer was South Dakota farmer P. Wendeloe. Not a trace of either of these historic machines exists today, though the old Hart-Parr Company and modern enthusiasts have undoubtedly looked everywhere for these machines.

With the success of those two machines, Hart and Parr were ready to put their prototype design into limited production. In 1903, the Hart-Parr Company turned out its first line of thirteen units.

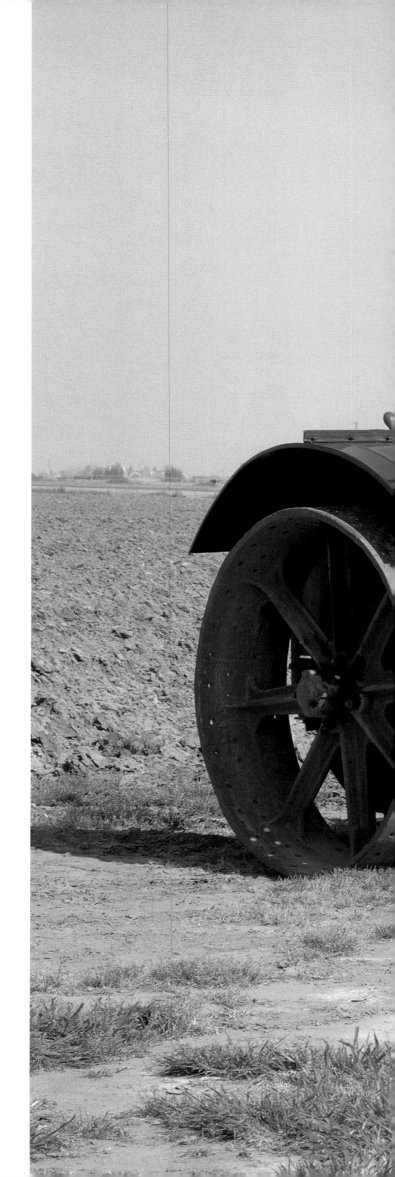

Big and clumsy compared to modern tractors, the new machines at that time looked dainty next to the big steamers. Interest in the new technology began to build when farmers watched these machines in the field. Seeing was believing. The power and reliability of the Hart-Parr machines were winning converts.

Besides the tractor and the modern assembly line, the Hart-Parr Company is credited with refining still another modern business concept: early product promotion. Hart and Parr were building product awareness while their first machines were still in pieces on the factory floor. The company had recruited a University of Wisconsin classmate, W. H. Williams, as its sales manager; his advertising for the Hart-Parr Tractor first appeared in the agricultural publication *The American Thresherman* in 1902. And while it is unlikely that he first coined the term "tractor," since some historians point out that a man named George Edwards first used the word in a patent application in 1890, it was Williams's advertisements that popularized the term, making "tractor" a household word.

The Hart-Parr tractor attracted a lot of attention. Sales were slow at first, but interest in the machines grew as tractors began to prove their usefulness and reliability. Hart-Parr machines were so well-designed that they soon earned the loving nickname "Old Reliable." By 1914 the company had added this new moniker to its advertising, reminding farmers that, regardless of all the newer and fancier tractors on the market, "Old Reliable" was the one to stick with.

*The 1927 Hart-Parr Model 28-50 was introduced just before the Depression years, and only about 450 were built. Age, scarcity and history make this machine especially desirable for collectors. This particular tractor belongs to Robbie Soults.*

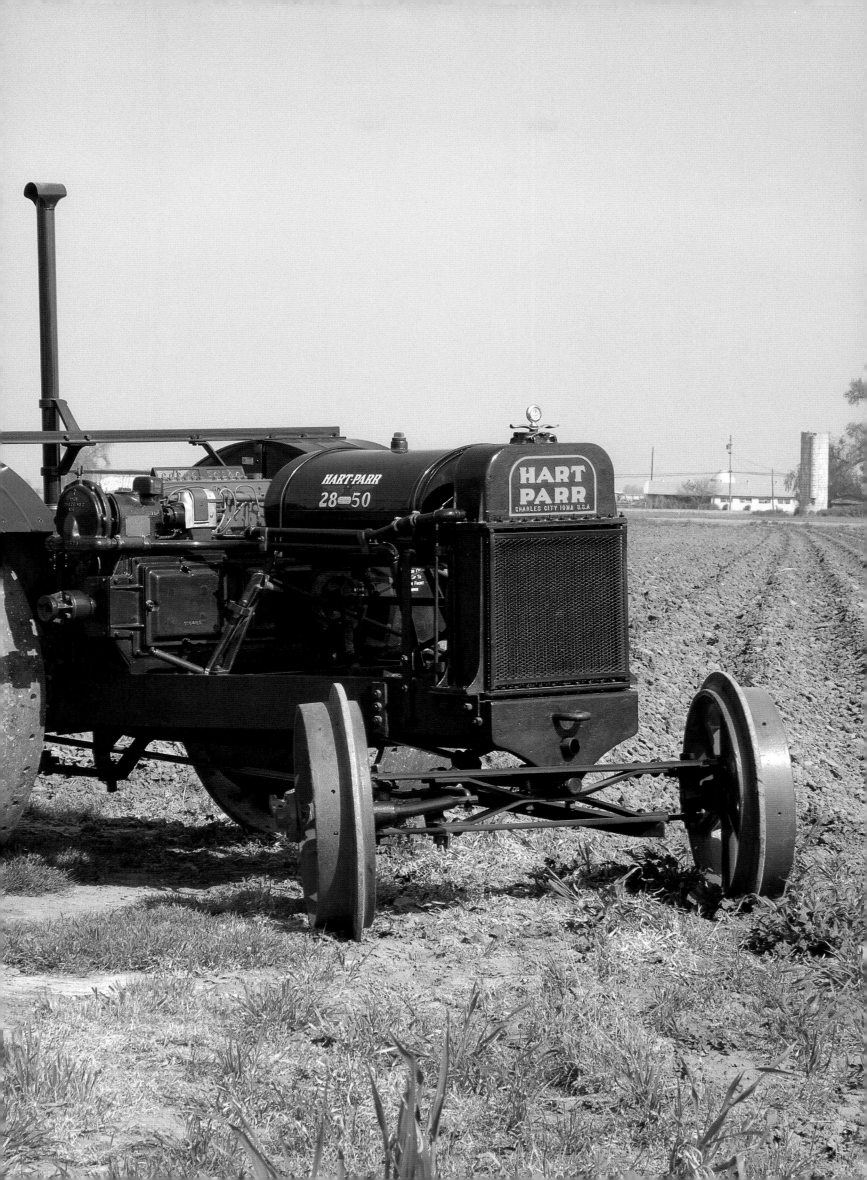

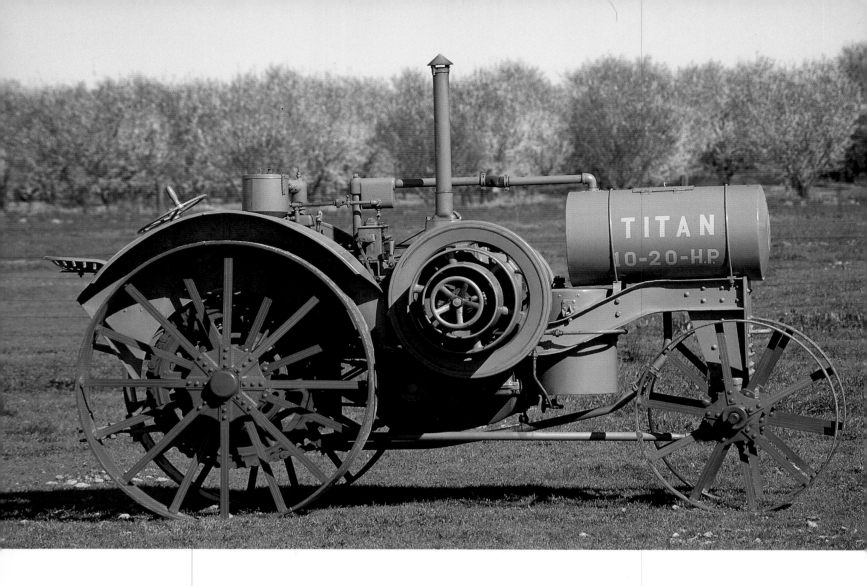

## Competition Heats Up

Hart-Parr had the market to itself for just a few years after the first production tractor, the Hart-Parr, appeared in 1903. The company ran into its first serious competition around 1908, when the giant agricultural-machine manufacturer International Harvester introduced its motor cultivator, the first machine with a technology known as a *friction drive*. This was an early type of transmission and an important innovation in itself, one that was subsequently copied and modified by other builders.

The motor cultivator was a dependable and useful machine, but enormously limited. It was only useful for cultivating, or what we would now describe as weeding. In general, farmers needed a machine to do two entirely different types of chores. They needed a tractor to pull implements—like a plow, a seeder, a weed cultivator—and a harvesting machine of some sort. In addition, the farmer needed to park his tractor in the field to use as a stationary engine to drive a threshing machine or some other piece of farm machinery.

The earliest Hart-Parr machines could do only one job or the other. They were limited in their applications, but had no serious challengers. Even though the motor cultivator could do only one job—cultivate the soil—it showed Hart-Parr executives that other agricultural-equipment builders could develop machines that the public would buy. Hart-Parr no longer had the tractor field to themselves.

Henry Ford was busy building automobiles about this time, and several inventive companies quickly marketed a way to convert the new Ford auto for use as a farm vehicle. A number of manufacturers sold cultivator "kits" that bolted onto the new family car. Known as "automobile plows," they were marginally successful.

Statistics from the Department of Agriculture estimate that there were about six hundred gasoline tractors in America in 1910, more than half of them built by Hart-Parr. But the rest came from nearly two dozen other builders, large and small. Clearly Hart-Parr was facing some challenges.

Who were these other builders? The biggest and most successful ones were old-line agricultural-equipment manufacturers with the money either to buy an innovative tractor design or the engineering talent to build one themselves: International Harvester, Ford, the J.I. Case Company, Massey-Harris, and Caterpillar were a few of the famous early names. Later on, John Deere would jump into the fray, too.

The most innovative machines however, were made by the smaller builders. Designer and business-man Henry M. Wallis, a former Case company executive, built the solid little Wallis Cub. The LaCrosse Tractor Company, located in LaCrosse, Wisconsin, was an innovator with its Happy Farmer tricycle tractor. A completely different type of machine was developed by the Cleveland Tractor Company, located in a Cleveland, Ohio, suburb. They built a crawler tractor known as the Cletrac, introducing their revolutionary machine just before World War I.

One of the most important early tractors came out in 1913 when the Bull Tractor Company intro-duced its "Little Bull," the first three-wheeled tractor ever seen. It was solid, maneuverable and affordable. Farmers quickly bought hundreds of these little machines, and the big builders scrambled to imitate

*BELOW: **One of the most interesting trac-tors still in existence, this extremely rare Track-Pull owned by California collector Bill Traill is thought to be the only example remaining. Designed for use in orchards and vineyards, the Track-Pull was an early offering of FMC, a pioneer builder of tracked vehicles. It originally appeared around World War I.***

the "Bull with the Pull," the first with the "tricycle" appearance that would char-acterize the tractor for many years. Sales figures for the Bull also demonstrated that farmers would buy thousands of tractors if it seemed to be a reliable machine. For the first time, competition in the mar-ketplace and the individual buyer began to determine the engineering of new tractors.

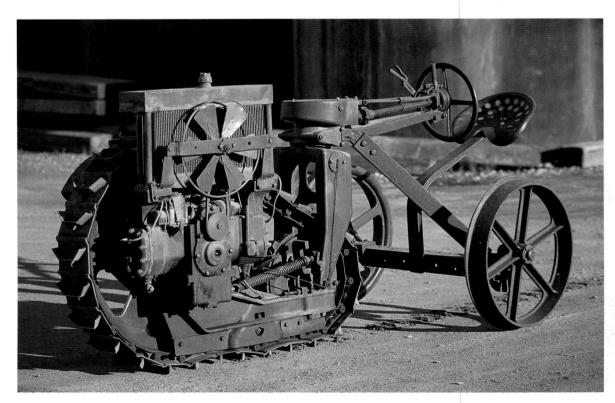

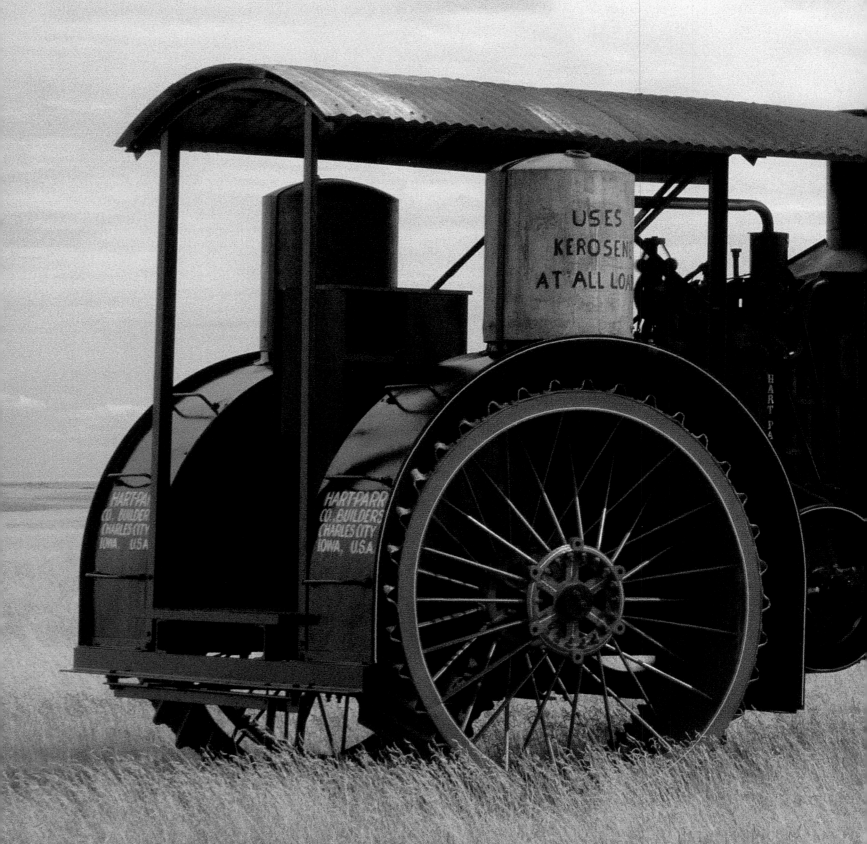

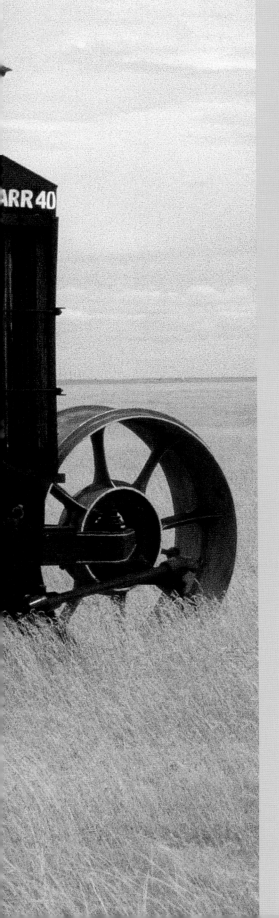

# HAPPY BIRTHDAY TO "OLD RELIABLE"

THE OLDEST TRACTOR IN AMERICA is in the collection of the Smithsonian Institution in Washington, D.C. Known as the Mitchell tractor, in honor of the pioneering farmer who first had the courage to buy this new machine, this early Hart-Parr tractor first appeared in 1903. It is thought to be the fourth tractor ever built. The tractor is not currently on display.

Until recently, the Mitchell tractor was shown in an agricultural museum near Cleveland, Ohio. Built by Hart-Parr during its first year of production, the Mitchell tractor was the focal point of an advertising campaign in the 1920s, when competition between early tractor builders began to really heat up.

The J.I. Case Company launched an advertising campaign centered on its famous Case trotting horse, Jay Eye Cee. Looking for a memorable alternative, the Hart-Parr Company promoted itself as the "Founders of the Tractor Industry," molding that title into the front of every tractor. In addition, Hart-Parr tracked down its earliest machine and restored it, featuring the machine at dozens of state fairs and exhibits. Known and advertised as "Old Reliable," this early line of tractors made Hart-Parr a legitimately successful company.

The Hart-Parr Company located its early machine in 1922, and Charles Parr himself began the restoration work on the tractor. After touring the country, the Mitchell tractor went on display at the Century of Progress exhibition in Chicago in 1933-1934. Then for ten years it was shown at Chicago's Museum of Science and Industry before being donated to the Smithsonian, around 1945.

Until recently, the Mitchell tractor was thought to be Hart-Parr tractor number three, the first production tractor the company built. Hart and Parr built two prototype machines first and sold them in 1903; then the partners built their first line of thirteen production machines. But historians Doug Strawser and Todd Stockwell recently looked more closely at the production records and the serial number stamped on the earliest version of "Old Reliable," and discovered that serial number 1207 identified the fourth machine built, not the third. At present, the fate and location of Hart-Parr tractor number three remains a mystery.

Today the world's oldest tractor has been returned to its home in the Smithsonian museum. Currently, it is housed in a Fullerton, Virginia, warehouse, the repository for many other historic artifacts that are not currently on display. The years have reportedly taken their toll, and there is some evidence that a few of the vital parts are now missing. Old Reliable needs a complete overhaul, top to bottom and inside out.

At present there are no plans to restore this historic machine. From time to time, there has been some talk about restoring the Hart-Parr tractor in time for the one hundredth anniversary of its birth. It would be wonderful to fire it up and roll it around a field just once more.

*It's as big as a steamer but don't let the size fool you. This is one of the earliest gas-powered tractors known, the Hart-Parr 22-40. It ran on a kerosene-type fuel known as distillate. Early models were huge but quickly evolved into the more compact machines we recognize as the modern tractor.*

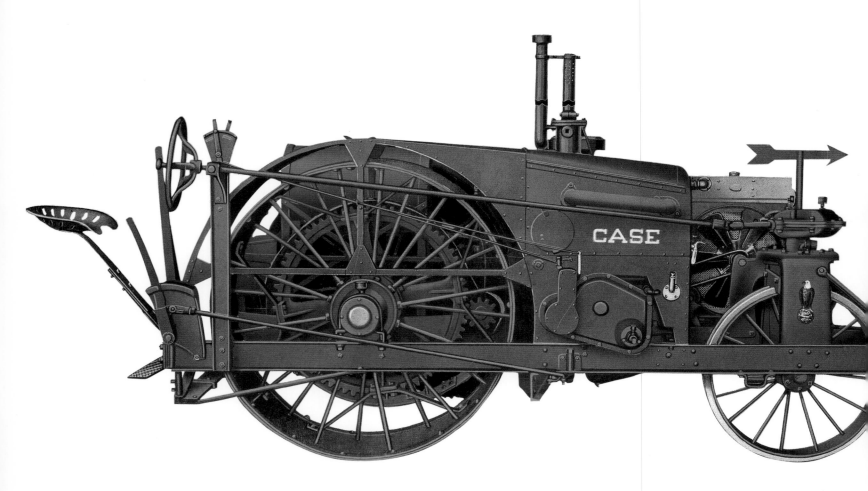

## J.I. Case Makes Its Case

The J.I. Case Company was a relative latecomer to the tractor game. A world leader in steam traction machines and threshers, the company feared that a gasoline tractor would rival their traditional product line. Case executives continued to stick with their proven and profitable winners, and built twenty-four thousand steam tractors after 1900, at a time when little tractor builders were springing up all over. When Case customers began asking for a tractor-type machine, the company obliged, offering a gasoline-powered traction machine in 1911. Predictably, the Case tractor looked much like the company's large, steam-powered models.

Case tractors were always expensive—they are sometimes referred to as the Cadillac of tractors—and the company was not known as an innovator in tractor design. But the machines Case built were extremely solid and reliable, qualities that were quite important in the farm area of the upper Great Plains and Canada, where Case had established its traditional customer base.

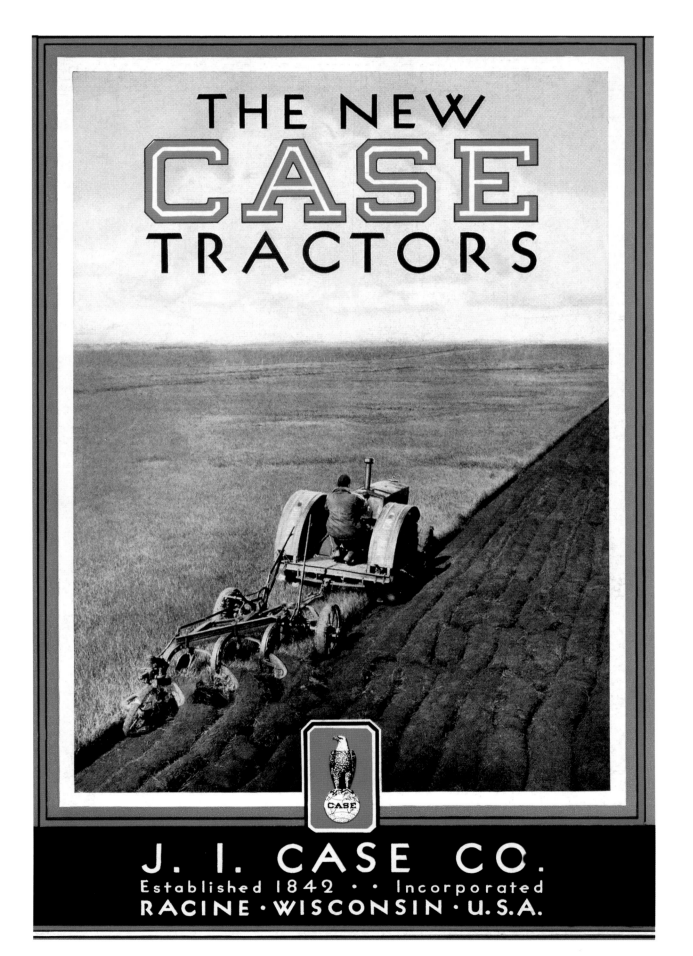

THE NEW
CASE
TRACTORS

J. I. CASE CO.
Established 1842 · · Incorporated
RACINE · WISCONSIN · U.S.A.

*FOLLOWING PAGES:*
*The Avery Tractor Company of Peoria, Illinois developed a machine that used oil rather than water as a coolant. The Avery 25-50 was introduced in 1914 and resembles some of the large old steamers. This machine belongs to Doug Peltzer and is essentially in original condition.*

*LEFT: The J.I. Case Company had established its reputation for excellent farm machinery when Case himself first started building and servicing threshers back in 1842. A long-time leader in the farm implement business, Case engineering and reliability helped turn their tractors into outstanding machines.*

39

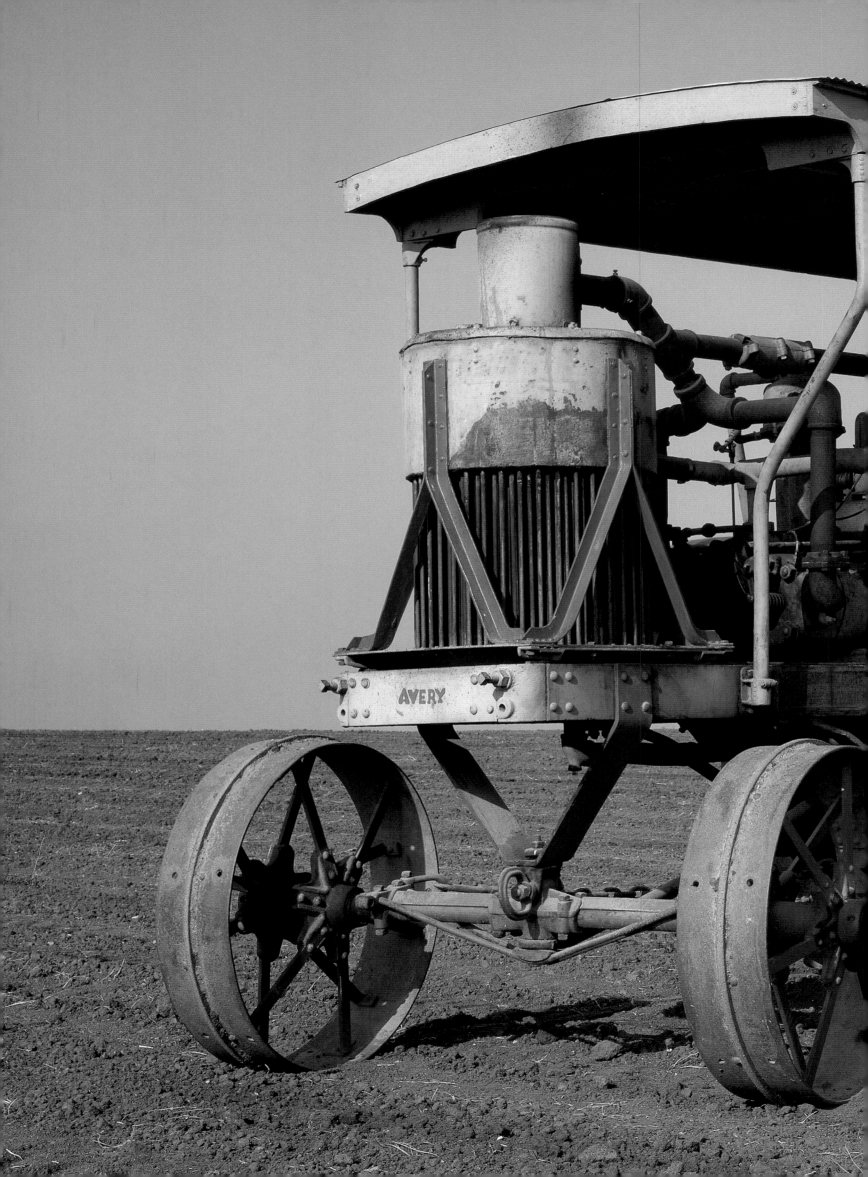

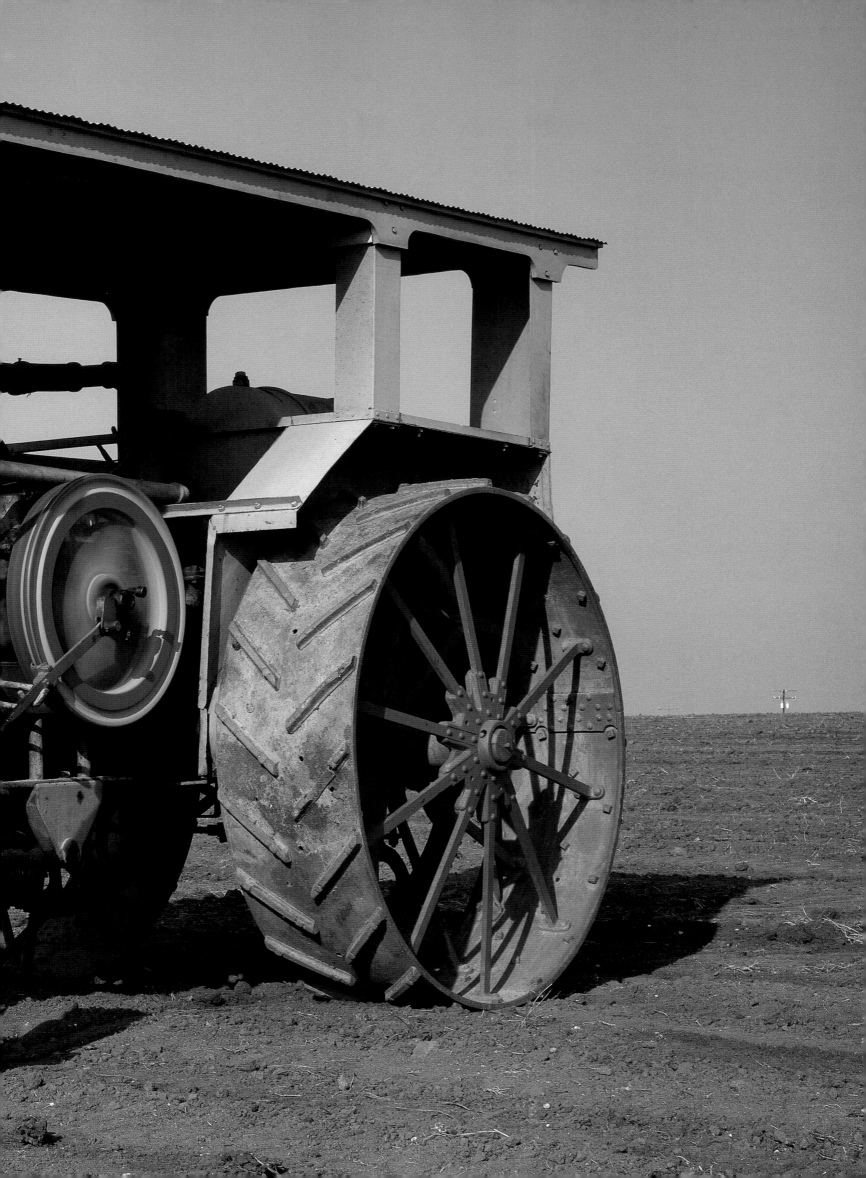

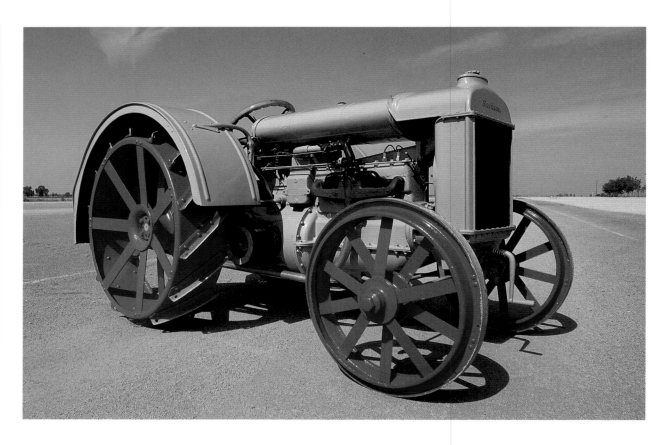

*RIGHT: **Early Fordson tractors, built by auto-maker Henry Ford and his son Edsel Ford, were known for being both uncomfortable and hot for the operator. Their greatest advantage was that they were cheap. This beautiful early Fordson is owned by the Kuckenbecker Tractor Company of Madera, California.***

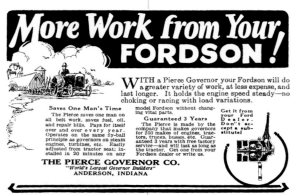

*ABOVE: **Eventually Fordson would improve the comfort and safety of its tractor. However, they steadfastly refused to sell implements for their machine, a situation that forced many farmers to buy from the competition in order to get equipment that was suitable.***

## The Fordson Blazes a Trail

By the end of World War I, agricultural manufacturers were faced with a new and formidable competitor: Henry Ford and his inexpensive Fordson tractor. Ford was a farm boy who grew up outside Dearborn, Michigan. As a youngster he hated the drudgery of farm chores, and long before he ever thought of building a motor car, he had wanted to build a tractor. After production of the Ford automobile was under way, Henry Ford turned his attention to his first love—tractors.

Ford had a prototype tractor working by 1907, and he wanted to go into the motor cultivator business, as the tractor business was then called, but the board of directors of the Ford Motor Company was adamantly opposed to that notion. The board wanted to build only automobiles and did not wish to compete with powerful agricultural conglomerates, such as International Harvester and J.I. Case, in the tractor business.

In great frustration, Ford resigned from his own company and started a new one. He named it Fordson, bringing his son Edsel into the business, and working on a mass-produced agricultural machine using the same principles he had pioneered in the auto industry. The Fordson tractor's great benefit was that it was cheap. It was not especially strong or reliable, but it was good enough and dependable enough.

Introduced in America in late 1917, reaction to the Fordson was mixed. The tractor seat was mounted directly over the worm gear, resulting in a very hot backside for the operator. Early Fordson tractors had a number of other problems, too, but in 1918 Ford built and sold 133,000 tractors, leading International Harvester in sales.

Recalling that his forebears had come from County Cork, Ireland, Ford went overseas and built his first tractor factory abroad. The Fordson was built in Ireland by the thousands and shipped to the European continent, where post–World War I farmers were desperate to get back on their feet. Ford tractors quickly became more popular in Europe than in the United States, where competition in the tractor field was still heated.

However, Henry Ford had changed the shape and purpose of the tractor, forcing all the traditional agricultural equipment companies to run to their drawing boards. Tractors now had to become light and maneuverable, and very, very cheap. The Fordson demonstrated that the farmer was willing to buy if the price was right. Other tractor builders took that lesson to heart.

## International Harvester's Farmall Does it All

Few tractor builders combined innovation and reliability as well as the International Harvester Company, whose roots stretch back to the middle of the nineteenth century. IH was known as a full-line implement dealer, offering the farmer everything from wagons to plows. Formed in 1902 by a merger of the McCormick and Deering Companies, these giants quickly acquired the assets of several smaller firms, including the American Harvesting Company. Because both McCormick and Deering were organizations with many equipment dealerships in their sales networks, each sold a different tractor despite the merger. McCormick had the Mogul tractor, and Deering sold a line of machines known as the Titan. Always eager to compete with giants like the J.I. Case Company, the new International Harvester Company continued to upgrade its two existing tractors, while continuing to offer its more traditional products, which included mowers and harvesting equipment.

*BELOW:* **Despite its somewhat ungainly look, with two big wheels in back and two tiny wheels placed together in front, farmers loved the Farmall immediately. It was first introduced in 1924 by International Harvester and, after a few improvements the following year, became a tremendous success.**

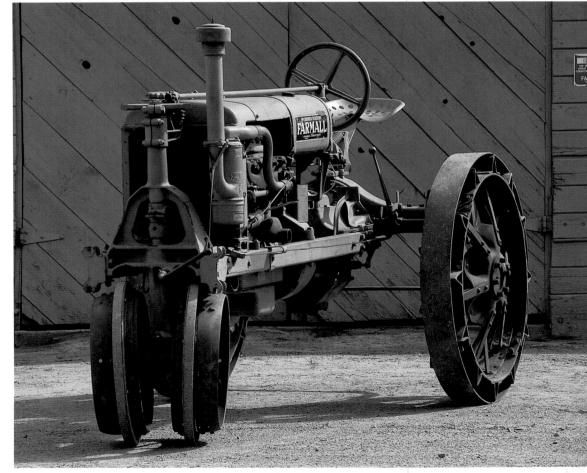

In the meantime, International's R & D people were working on designs for a third tractor, one to compete with Ford.

The engineers at IH had experimented with a motor cultivator between 1915 and 1918. With the Fordson taking away market share, IH now found it critical to develop a tractor of its own—its corporate reputation as a market leader simply demanded a new machine. The IH solution was a wonderful machine with an innovative device built into the engine. Called the "power take-off," or PTO, it was a simple, rotating shaft, sticking out the bottom of the tractor in the rear, and was powered directly from the tractor engine. This shaft could easily be connected to all sorts of farm implements, providing a power source to operate them as the tractor pulled them across the field.

International Harvester introduced this innovative tractor in 1924. Dubbing it the Farmall, the company exalted it as the only tractor the farmer would need—the machine that "could perform all the farm tasks except milking." The extremely versatile and adaptable machine lived up to its lofty promise, and quickly became the favorite tractor of many farmers. The wonderful addition of the PTO now allowed all sorts of power-driven implements to be connected directly to the tractor. No longer was it necessary to provide a separate power source for binding hay, for example—the PTO provided all the power necessary for that operation. What's more, the PTO enabled farmers to operate implements while they drove the tractor around their fields. Before the introduction of the PTO, the tractor had to be stationary and the various pieces of equipment had to be belted up to the tractor's flywheel.

The Farmall's distinctive shape proved very popular with farmers. Tall, spindly, and gangly, it resembled a tricycle, with two tiny wheels close together in front and two large wheels in back. This configuration enabled farmers to make tighter turns, providing greater agility between crop rows. By contrast, the Fordson and the Case machines were boxy and square, looking more like automobiles.

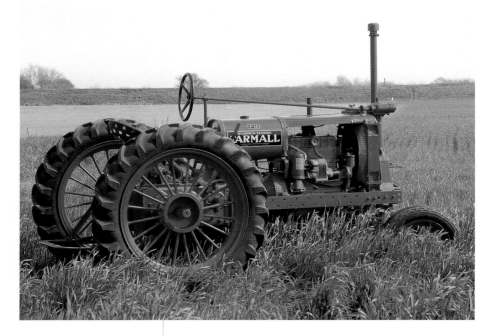

*BELOW: Looking a lot like an earlier Farmall, this Model F-14 was introduced late in the Depression, in 1938. Anxious to compete, tractors from International Harvester were all painted bright red. This one is owned by Denis Van de Maele.*

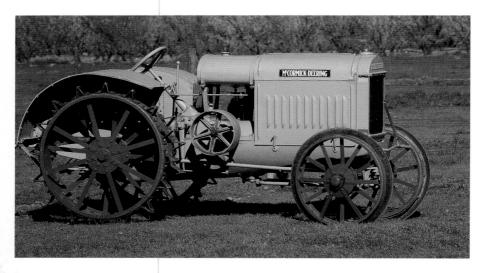

*ABOVE: McCormick-Deering was the company that the early Ford Motor Company feared—and with good reason. Tough, powerful tractors such as this Model 10-20, were heavy competition for the light-weight Fordson.*

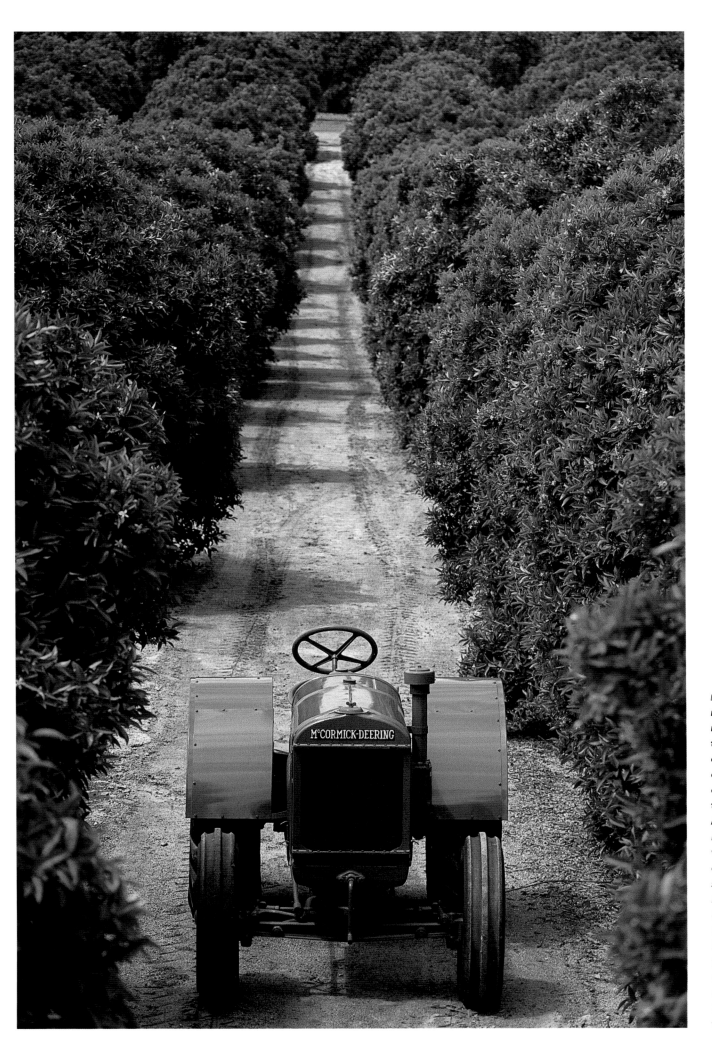

*LEFT:* **Most tractor makers built a few machines designed to serve the specialized needs of customers such as orchardists. Orchard tractors, like this McCormick-Deering, have wide fenders and extremely low seats so that the machines are able to maneuver under overhanging branches. Always few in number, orchard tractors are especially rare. This one belongs to Doug Peltzer.**

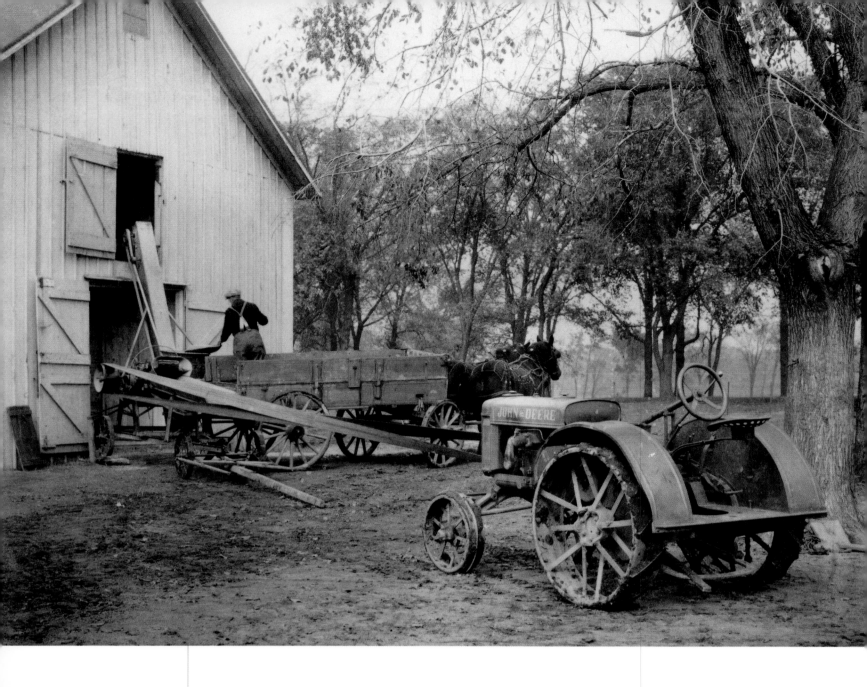

## The Birth of a Favorite: The John Deere Tractor

Tractors were but a small part of the catalog of venerable plow maker and agricultural equipment dealer John Deere. It would be many years before the John Deere Company would become the tremendous contender in the tractor market that it is today. Although the company had tried developing a tractor of its own starting in 1912, it really entered the tractor market in 1918, when it bought the Waterloo Gasoline Engine Company of Waterloo, Iowa, makers of the Waterloo Boy tractor. Overnight, John Deere was in the tractor business. The company was quick to make the improvements needed to keep its Waterloo machines in step with the competition.

In 1924—the same year that International Harvester debuted its Farmall—John Deere released what was to be one of the most popular and beloved tractors of all time, the John Deere Model D. This model was sold for nearly thirty years, its longevity a testimony to its popularity. A relatively small tractor with a two-cylinder engine, the Model D was extremely rugged and reliable. Its simplicity made it extremely popular with farmers, most of whom did their own maintenance. Finally, the average farmer had a good, small, inexpensive machine that was both reliable and versatile.

## Caterpillar and Cletrac

An entirely different type of tractor appeared in the field around 1904. The Holt Manufacturing Company of Stockton, California, built its first crawler in the 1890s, but it was several years before the machine that is now familiar to us all came on the scene. Laying eyes on the curious treaded machine for the first time, farmers were apt to say, "It looks like a caterpillar!" The name stuck and was patented.

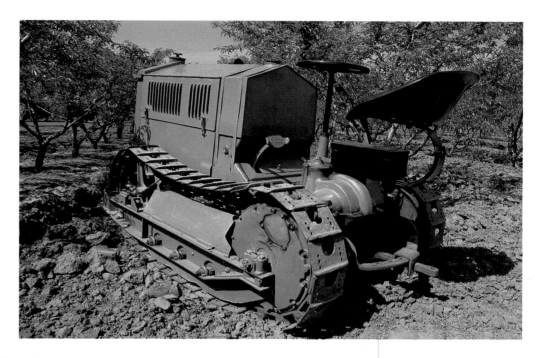

Caterpillar and later crawler tractors such as the Cletrac are an important part of the tractor industry, and new tractor enthusiasts are usually surprised to learn that these wonderful machines debuted so early in tractor history.

The crawler solved some special problems for the farmer. It was tremendously strong and could be built to deliver more than a hundred horsepower. Only the earlier steam engines could produce that much muscle. Unlike wheeled tractors, whose high centers of gravity were inclined to cause them to roll over or flip, crawlers were very stable. And crawlers could operate in damp, sandy, or boggy soils—farmland

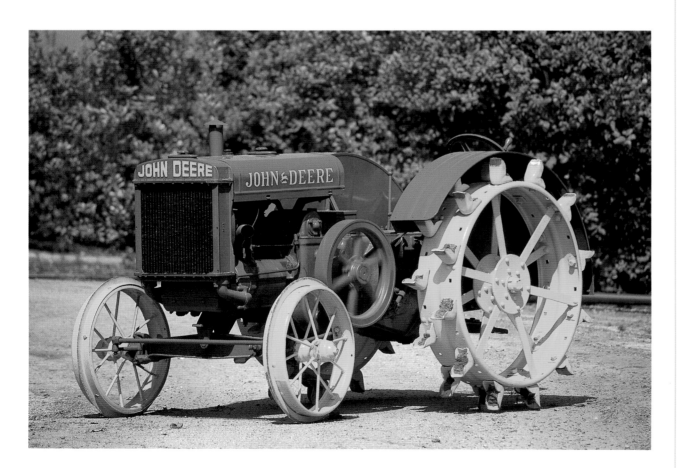

*ABOVE:* **It's difficult to believe that the little Cletrac, which was first introduced in 1915, always maintained the same basic form. It was hard to improve on perfection and this little workhorse was an immediate best seller. This impeccable early model is owned by the Bechthold family.**

*LEFT:* **John Deere tractors quickly became all-time favorites. The Model D was produced for over thirty years, and proved to be extremely versatile. Farmers liked its simplicity and economy and its two-cylinder engine was easy to maintain.**

that had always posed problems for farmers using the traditional agricultural methods involving horses or steam machinery.

Crawlers were developed in California and were particularly well suited for farming in the California delta. First appearing in San Leandro and then manufactured in Stockton, crawlers proved quite useful not only for farm work but for all sorts of large construction jobs. Suitable for heavy tasks like road building and house moving, no job seemed too big or too tough for these versatile machines.

The improved Caterpillar crawler was a remarkable piece of machinery, produced from a rivalry and then the subsequent 1908 merger between the Best Manufacturing Company of San Leandro, California, and the Holt Manufacturing Company of Stockton, California. Holt and Best were two early western companies, both builders of agricultural implements. Both companies started building steam tractors around 1885 and the two were keen competitors.

Perhaps it was inevitable that the two agricultural manufacturers, both designing and producing large-scale machinery, would become rivals. The two factories were located about fifty miles apart, but the two were competing for the same customers: California wheat farmers with thousands of acres under cultivation.

Competition led to lawsuits. Daniel Best sued Benjamin Holt, charging patent infringement, but several years of litigation and appeals enriched only their attorneys. The two compromised and, in 1908, Best sold his company to Holt for $325,000. Members of the Best family went to work for Holt.

But after two years, Clarence L. Best, a son of the founder of the Best Manufacturing Company, decided to build his own crawler, which he named the Tracklayer. Under terms of the merger agreement, C.L. Best was forbidden from entering the tractor business for ten years, but he ignored the pact and forged ahead, making Holt and Best rivals once again. This time, however, innovative engineering and thorough patent research kept C.L. Best out of court.

Always looking for publicity, Best took his Tracklayers to the Panama-Pacific International Exposition, a big world's fair held in San Francisco in 1915, where businessman from Cleveland named Rollin White spotted one. An heir to the White sewing-machine fortune, Rollin immediately saw tremendous possibilities and tried to interest

*BELOW: **Crawlers are noted for their extreme stability and their ability to turn on their own axis. In addition, a crawler can pull a weight equal to its own, a tremendous advantage over a conventional tractor. Small crawlers such as the Cletrac, built by the Cleveland Tractor Company, have always sold well.***

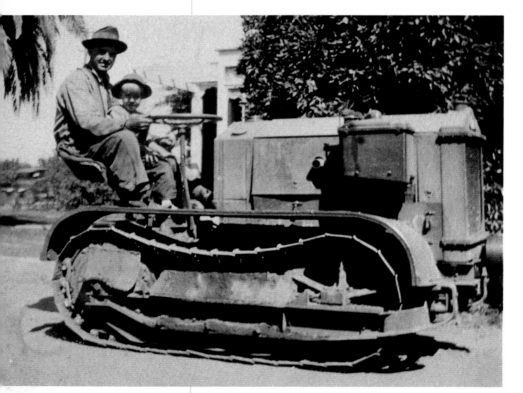

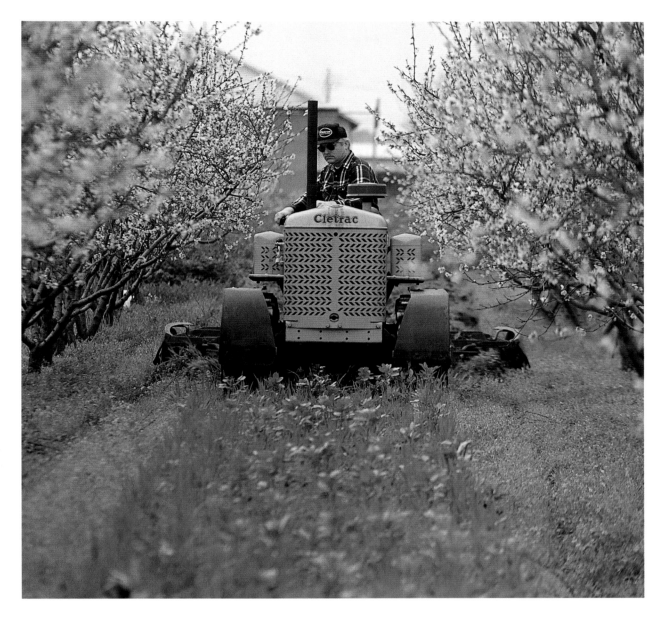

LEFT: **The front grille changed but little else had to be redesigned on the Cletrac. Crawlers were designed for use in sandy soils that would prove treacherous to conventional tractors. Bill Bechthold uses his vintage Cletrac in his Lodi, California, orchard.**

BELOW: **The Caterpillar trademark was registered in 1910 to describe a machine designed nearly twenty years earlier. This amazing design was developed for the swampy soils of the California delta but has proven to have important applications for military tanks and the construction industry.**

Best in a business arrangement in which White would build a factory and manufacture the crawler, licensing the design. Best was not interested. He turned down White, as well as his corporate sales manager, C. L. Hawkins, but later made a crucial tactical error. Always short of operating cash, Best agreed to sell one of his demonstration models from the floor of the exposition to Rollin White.

White took the Tracklayer model home to Cleveland, copying the design and rebuilding it, and changed some critical elements in the track system. White named his new, modified machine the Cletrac. He then set up the Cleveland Tractor Company to build his machine and, in 1916, presold twelve thousand Cletracs on the basis of a brochure and a photograph. It was such a solid machine, so useful and so versatile, that the basic design remained the same until the Cletrac company was bought out by the Oliver Tractor Company in 1944.

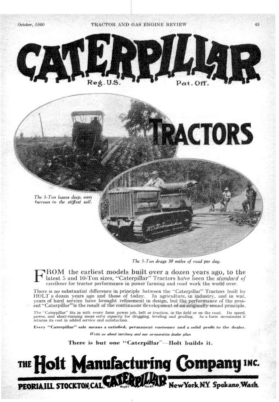

49

*BELOW: The first Heider tractor was patented in 1911 and proved to be an early success. Overwhelmed by orders, the little company contacted a larger manufacturer for help with manufacture and distribution. Rock Island continued to build and sell the Heider until 1927.*

Crawlers have some wonderful virtues and most of the larger tractor builders still have a line of crawlers in their product catalogs. Enormously stable on slopes, crawlers have proven themselves as the machine of choice in hillside orchards. They have tremendous power for their size and can pull a load equal to their own weight. And they are able to turn on a dime, pivoting completely around within their own length. All these attributes make them a favorite machine of many farmers.

Thus, during the 1920s, tractors really began to come into their own. Farmers started to realize what a wonderful and versatile machine a tractor could be. The only factor limiting tractor use was the

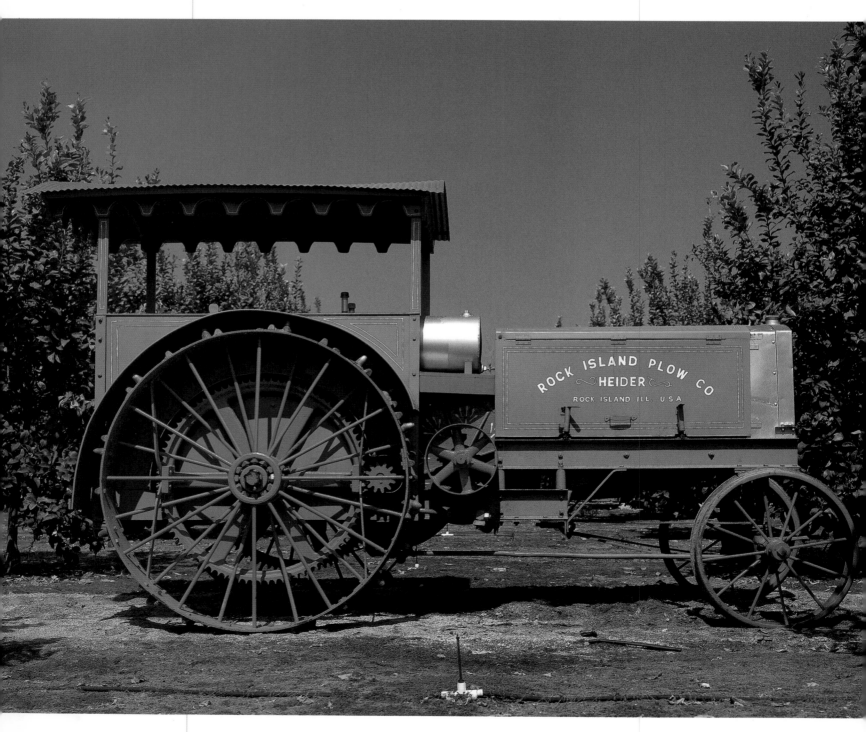

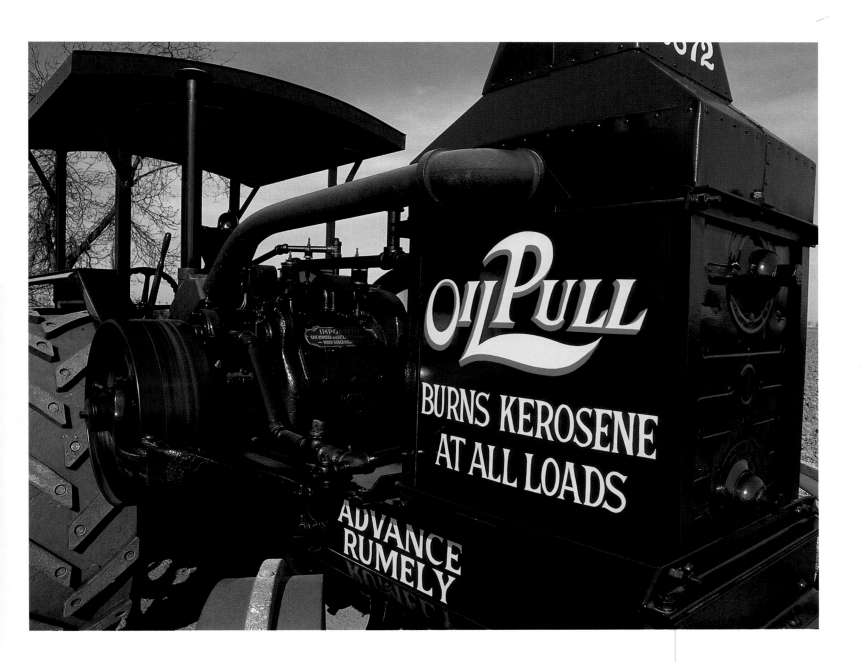

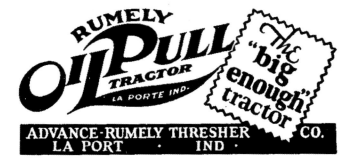

WHEN WRITING ADVERTISERS PLEASE

*ABOVE AND LEFT:*
**Advance-Rumely was originally a thresher builder that also manufactured steam engines. They started building the Oilpull in 1906 and manufactured over 56,000 in fourteen different models. Tractor production ended in 1931. The model above dates from 1910.**

51

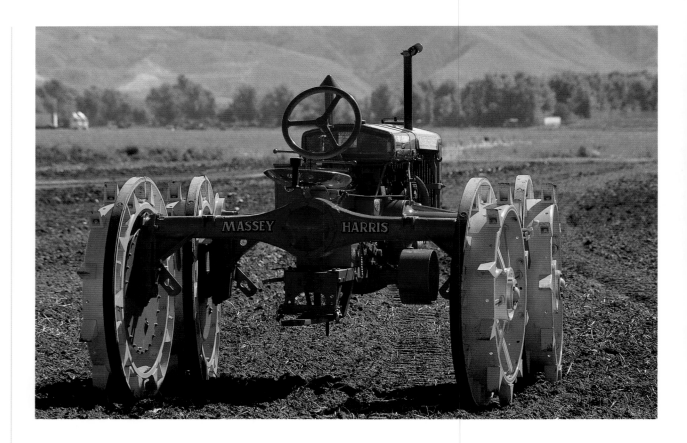

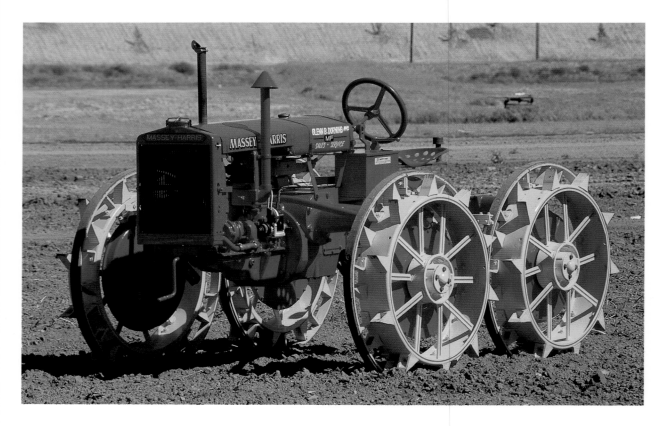

availability of fuel. The average farm tractor ran on what is known as distillate, a type of kerosene fuel that was hard to come by early in the twentieth century. But just as the fuel distribution system was becoming established nationwide, tractors were becoming better and cheaper. Fuel was getting easier for farmers to find. The promises of *Power Farming* were beginning to be realized. But the dark days of the Great Depression were just around the corner.

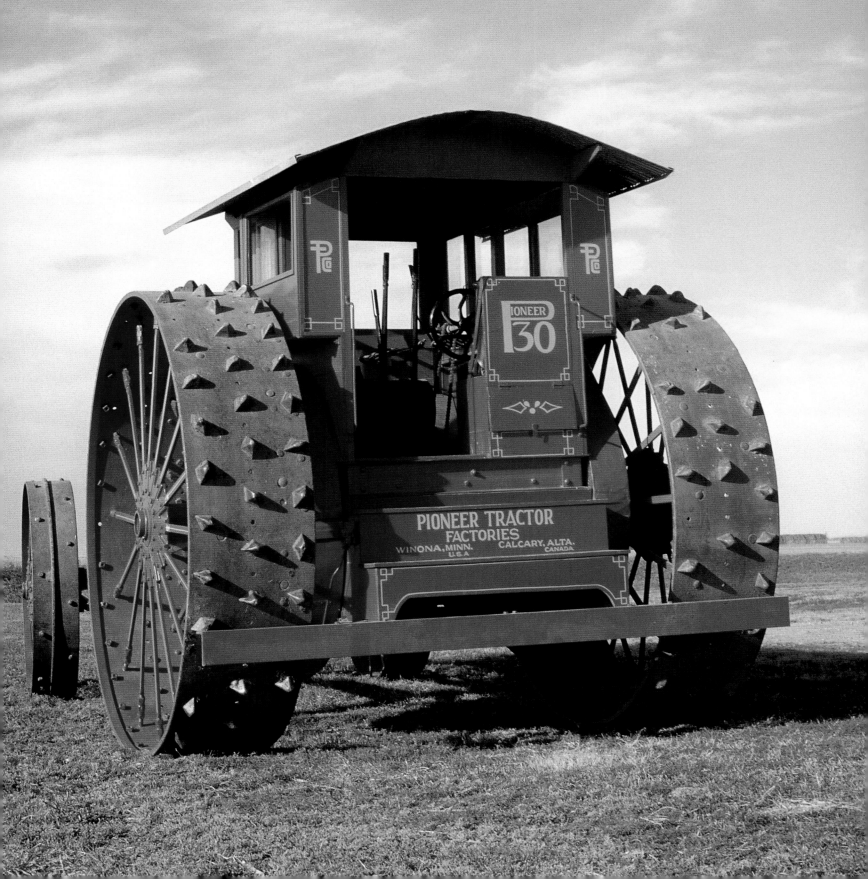

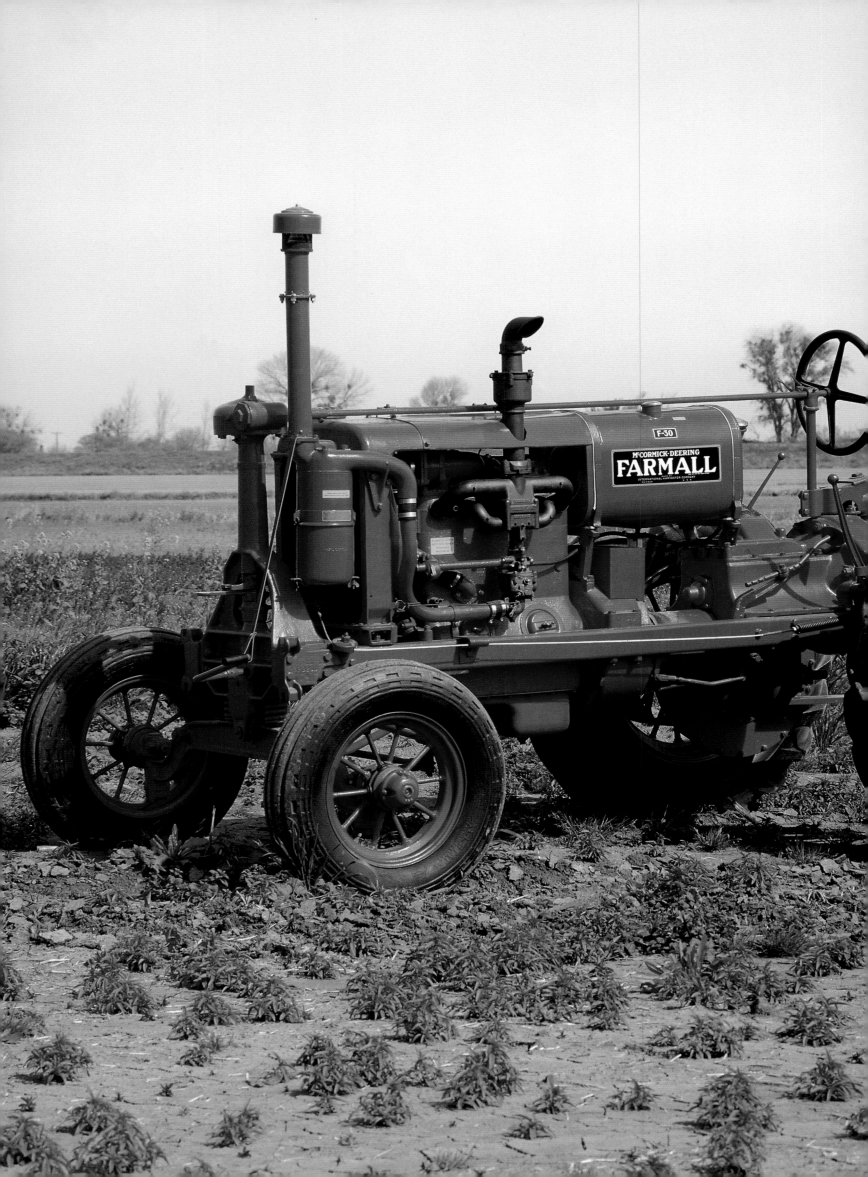

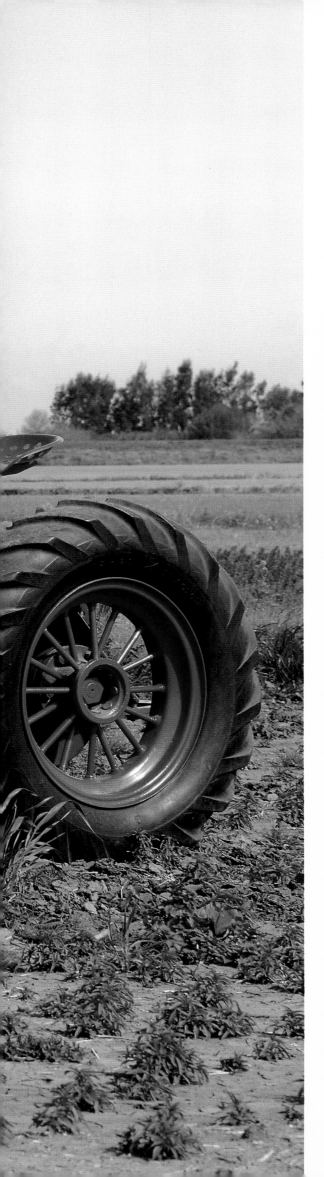

# HARD TIMES AND TOUGH BUILDERS

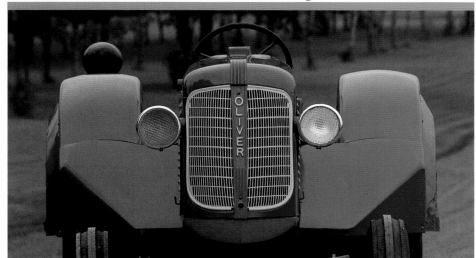

## Chapter Three

**D**uring the 1930s and early 1940s, the United States was rocked by the Great Depression and World War II. Each of those tumultuous events left an indelible impression on American society, economics, and culture. During the hard times of the Depression, farmers and tractor manufacturers suffered along with the rest of the nation. About fifty tractor builders were operating at the beginning of 1930, but only the strongest survived through the end of the decade. When the United States became involved in World War II in 1941, those few remaining tractor builders quickly realized that their industry was going to have to change once more.

With the war effort in full swing, men were diverted from the fields and factories to join the fight for the Allies. Raw materials and machinery that might have been used to build tractors were now needed to produce tanks,

*LEFT:* **The Farmall-30, on the market in 1936, offered bright paint and rubber tires. These small improvements helped revive sagging sales.**

*ABOVE:* **The sleek styling and outstanding new features of the Oliver rocked the entire tractor industry in 1935.**

fighter planes, and bombs. It was apparent that American farmers would have to mechanize if they were to continue providing enough food to feed the country. Hundreds of farm boys were drafted and the few who were left behind had to become a lot more productive. Hired help—always hard to find—totally disappeared, and many farm wives ran the farms when their husbands went to war. Reliable and easy-to-drive tractors would make all the difference.

## The Depression

The year 1929 ushered in the Great Depression, a time of record business failures. Farmers suffered, too, particularly in the area that was later known as the Dust Bowl. Large areas of the South- and Midwest, such as Oklahoma and Texas, had suffered several years of drought. Farmers watched their dry, sandy soil blow and drift like snow, sometimes completely covering their houses. Several dry years forced many farmers to abandon their homes and move in search of some sort of living for their families. As a result of the drought and the Depression, few farmers could buy new tractors, so demand all but disappeared.

By 1930, International Harvester controlled more than fifty percent of the tractor market. John Deere was in a distant second place with about twenty percent. Five or six builders divided the remainder into small pieces. The Depression was taking its toll on all sorts of businesses. Hundreds of small builders—plus the inventors, mechanics, and salesmen who once formed the backbone of companies like Twin Cities, Keck-Gonnerman, Huber Manufacturing, Eagle Manufacturing, and Foote Brothers—saw their livelihoods simply vanish. Some builders were lucky: they were consolidated, sold, or folded into larger corporations. The unlucky ones succumbed to bankruptcy.

Although the tractor business suffered greatly during the early 1930s, midway through the decade a marvelous and innovative design appeared that injected new life into an otherwise dull industry. Known to enthusiasts as "the prettiest tractor ever built," it was also one of the most innovative. The Oliver Tractor Company, heir to the Hart-Parr tradition, developed the machine that would be the industry leader for decades to come.

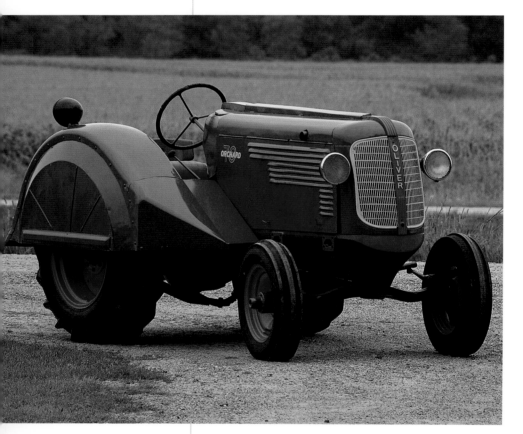

*BELOW: Oliver produced fewer than nine hundred of the Model 70 during 1945 and only a few of those machines ended up as orchard tractors like this one. This beautifully styled Oliver is in the collection of Everett Jensen. Oliver was always an extremely innovative tractor builder and this is a gorgeous demonstration of their craftsmanship.*

The Oliver 70 was not only a beautiful machine; it was a new machine, back to front and inside out. It had a new six-cylinder engine and it was powered by a new fuel: gasoline. Until the Oliver 70, tractors used a kerosene-type fuel; now for the first time a tractor could run on 70-octane gasoline, the same regular fuel that was widely distributed for use in motor cars. This important improvement gave the tractor its name.

In addition, the Oliver 70 had many other features that were now standard on the average automobile: rubber tires, electric headlights, a muffler, an electric starter, and a four-speed transmission. A high-compression engine could roll this little beauty along a highway at speeds of up to fourteen miles an hour. The Row-Crop model of the Oliver 70 featured an automatic starter and a powered implement lift.

New inside and out, the Oliver was the first "styled" tractor, a machine with a streamlined appearance, an aerodynamic shape reminiscent of the sleek styling of an airplane or an expensive automobile. The frame featured a continuous casting and the entire assemblage was a thing of sculptural beauty.

Finally, the designers of the Oliver 70 (thought by many to be brothers Herman and Rudolph Altgelt) developed an entirely new way of attaching implements to a tractor. On traditional tractors, the plows, cultivators, and seeders were hitched to the rear and pulled along behind. This meant that farmers had to constantly turn around and look over their shoulders, checking behind them. In addition, pulling an implement required a large turning radius at the end of a row.

But the Oliver Row-Crop machines offered an entirely new system of attaching implements, one whereby the implement was secured through the frame of the tractor. Thus, the tractor itself was

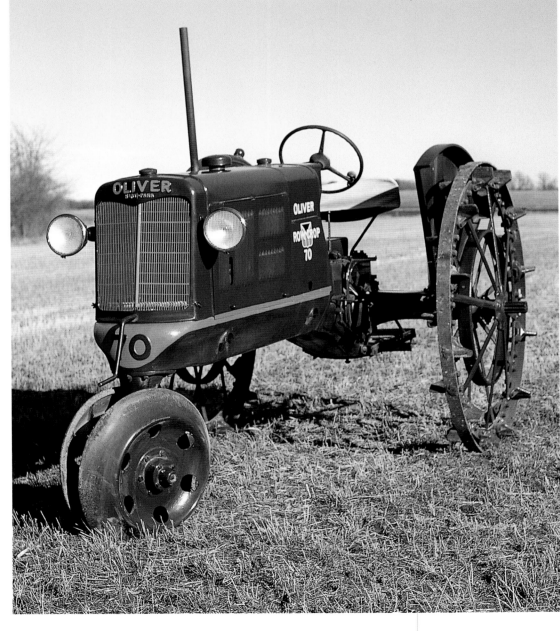

now an integral part of the implement, and, in many cases, farmers could just look down by their feet to check their work. Putting the implement under the frame also required a much smaller turning radius at the end of rows. In short, the new Oliver tractors were a dream come true.

A tremendous scramble ensued to catch up to the Oliver: the other builders spent the next couple of years modifying their tractors to compete. On the whole, though, the reaction was wonderful, benefiting the American farmer and providing better, cheaper machines even during what is usually considered the black times of the Depression.

## The Farmall Gets an Overhaul

One of the first tractor builders to react to the Oliver challenge was International Harvester. IH had to protect its share of the market and its image as the industry leader. Wasting no time, IH executives called in the biggest gun in the country, designer Raymond Loewy. The first change that IH made was to repaint its dull, gray Farmall tractor a bright, fiery red. It became a signature color, making their machines stand out.

Raymond Loewy was one of a new group of designers of the 1930s. Known as industrial designers, they were changing the shape of American products as well as the way America looked at design. They bestowed their magic touch on consumer goods of every kind. Packaging and furniture changed. Automobiles, airplanes, and locomotives all began to take on a sleek, aerodynamic appearance.

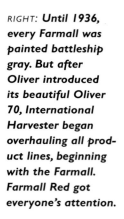

*RIGHT:* **Until 1936, every Farmall was painted battleship gray. But after Oliver introduced its beautiful Oliver 70, International Harvester began overhauling all product lines, beginning with the Farmall. Farmall Red got everyone's attention.**

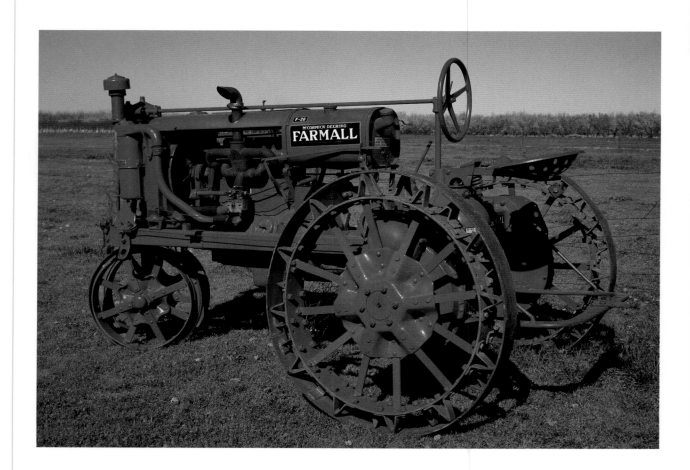

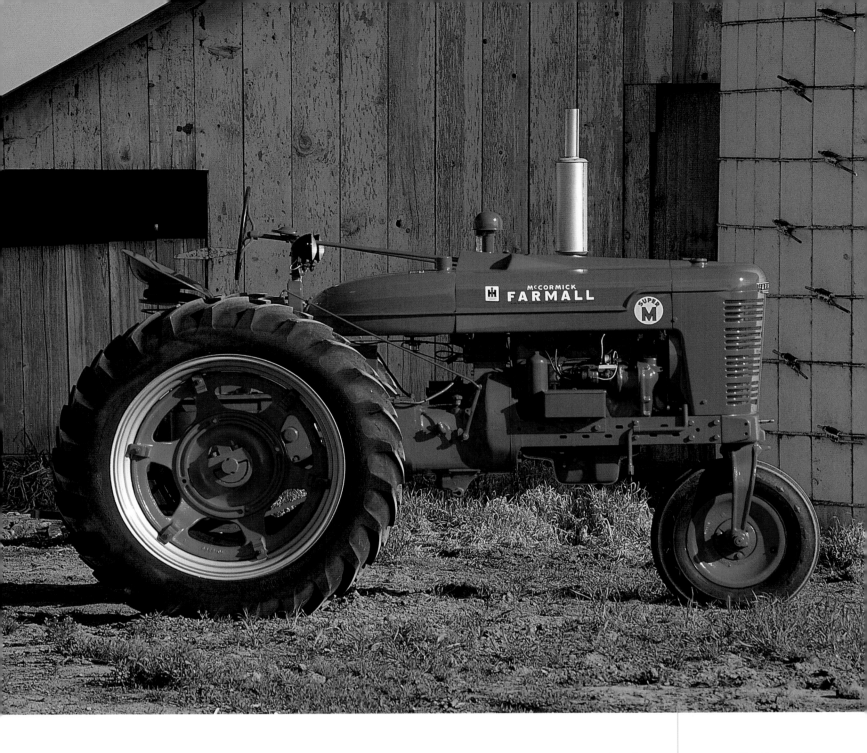

Loewy was noted for his daring design of the Studebaker car, an innovative shape that was immediately imitated by many manufacturers.

Loewy worked his styling magic on the Farmall, creating a distinctly rounded grille and smoothing its sheet metal. He redesigned the entire machine, creating a new logo and reworking the machine from the ground up. The older models in the product line received the new styling and a new paint job as well. But Loewy also brought his ability as an industrial designer to a new level when he broke with tradition and produced the Farmall A, introduced in 1939.

The Farmall A was the first tractor that put the driver to the side of the tractor. For years the farmer sat directly behind the engine, squarely in the middle. Now both the driver's seat and the steering wheel were offset to the left, as in the family sedan. This gave farmers an unobstructed view of the ground they would be cultivating. Loewy called his concept *cultivision*, and the new, off-center design proved to be extremely popular with farmers who were growing all sorts of row crops.

*ABOVE: **The Farmall M was produced from 1939 to 1952. It was completely new, responding to the Oliver challenge, and its sleek styling and tremendous performance gave Farmall owners great pride. The Model M was the largest member of an entire new family of Farmall models, denoted as A, B, C, H, and M.***

## Deere Redesigns

Since International Harvester had contracted with Loewy, Deere went looking for help from an equally famous industrial designer and ended up with Henry Dreyfuss. Dreyfuss had designed aircraft for Lockheed and telephones for the Bell System. He would help redesign the Deere to compete with the other industry leaders.

The Deere Company also decided to bring out several new models in a full range of sizes, one for every farm or

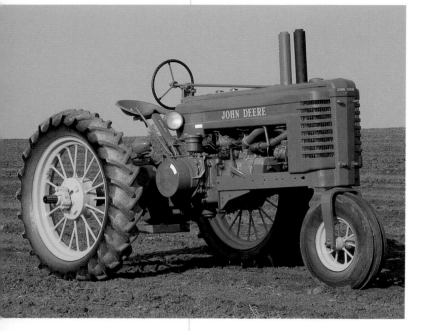

*BELOW: **John Deere also changed its styling and opted for a more aerodynamic appearance. Deere owners appreciated the versatility of the new design, which allowed the wheels to be adapted for different crops.***

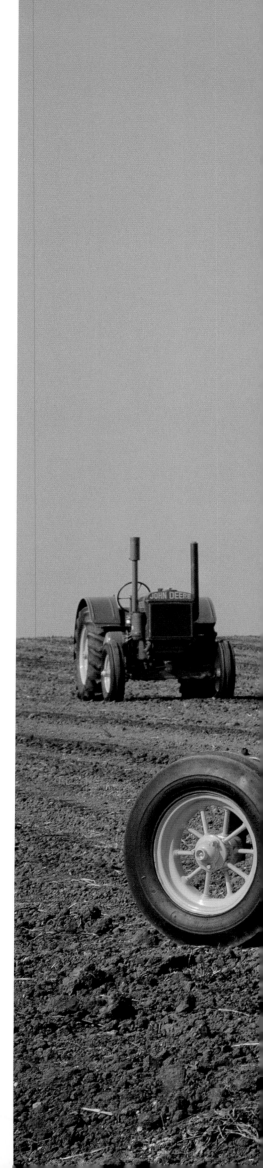

pocketbook. Since the introduction of the Oliver, a tractor now needed to be "stylish" to sell well. So Deere also entered the age of the styled tractor, and countered *cultivision* with its own updated version, the John Deere Model L.

Sometimes called the "Little" or the "Light," the Model L was a small tractor with offset steering to give the farmer greater visibility. Appearing in 1937, it was Deere's first direct response to International Harvester. A newly designed Model H, offered by John Deere in 1939, was larger than the "Little," which many considered suitable only for yard work. The Deere Company had already introduced its new Model G about the time that Dreyfuss was first contacted. So the Model G escaped the stylistic makeover for a few years, but it, too, came in for a complete overhaul by 1942.

Of all the machines that John Deere produced during the war years, the Model H was probably the most popular

*OPPOSITE: **John Deere, the old and the new. Built between 1937 and 1953, the General Purpose was Deere's most powerful tractor. Its most direct competition was probably the Farmall M, a machine with a four-cylinder engine. Both machines are from Doug Peltzer's collection.***

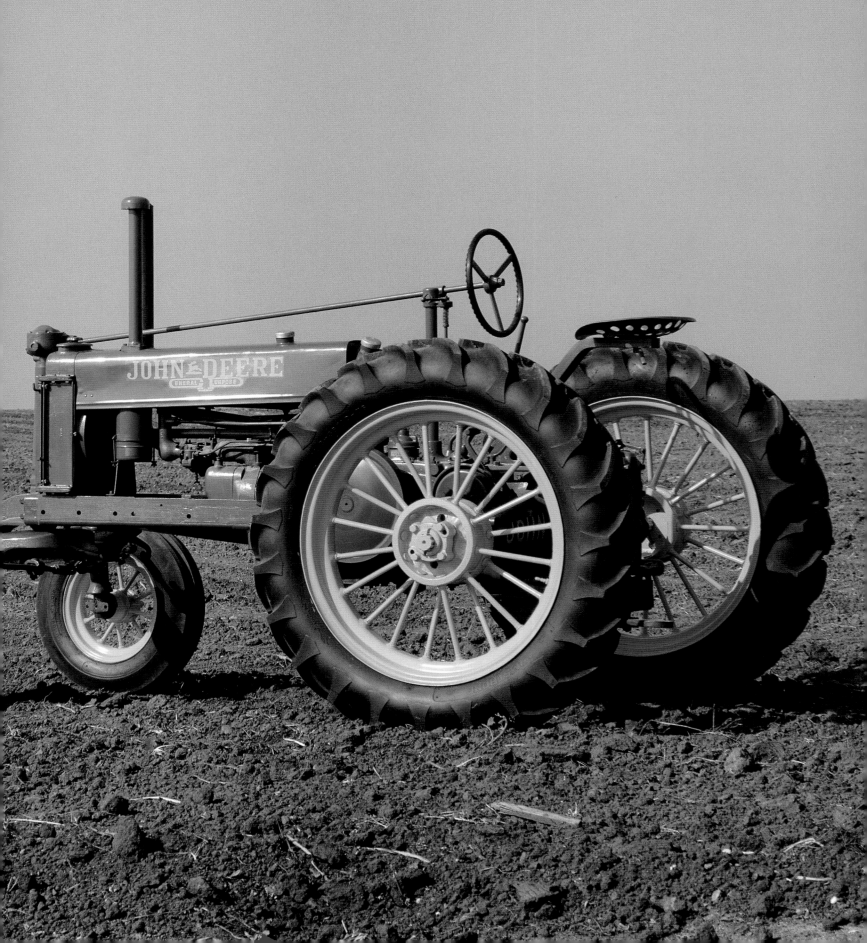

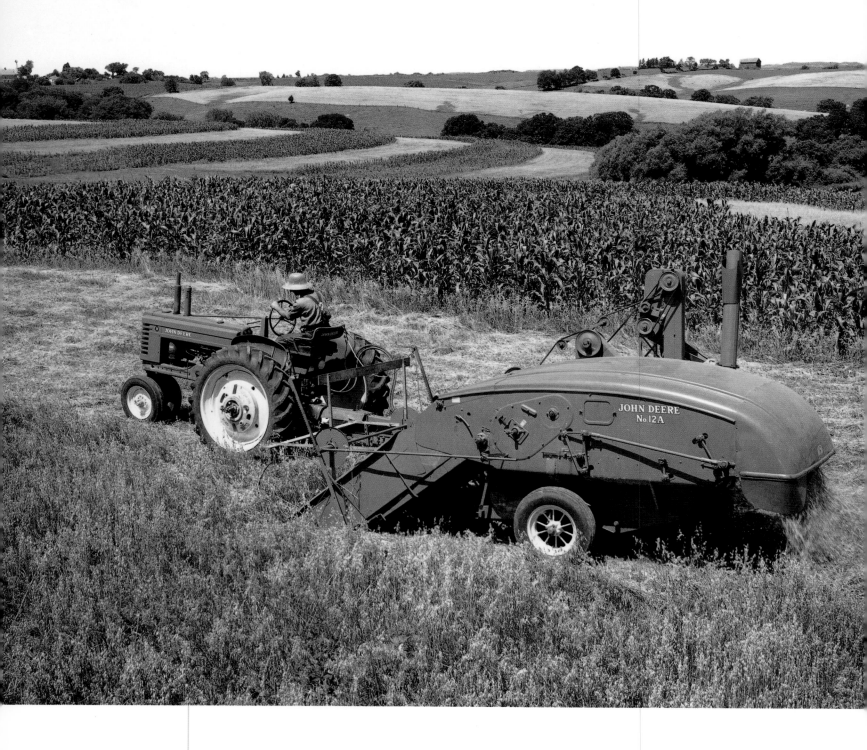

and the most versatile. Like other John Deere tractors, it could be ordered with options to meet each farmer's needs. The axles could be widened, the wheels could be raised or lowered, and additional optional configurations could be chosen to meet virtually any possible field situation and condition.

One other historic John Deere machine made its debut during these years: the crawler, known as the Lindeman or the Lindeman B. The Lindeman Company in Yakima, Washington, bought about two thousand John Deere Model B tractors and converted them to crawlers for use in West Coast orchards. Deere was happy with the change in configuration, since it had no crawler in its catalog to offer customers. At the end of the war, Deere finally bought out Lindeman and eventually offered a crawler of its own, known as the Deere Model MC.

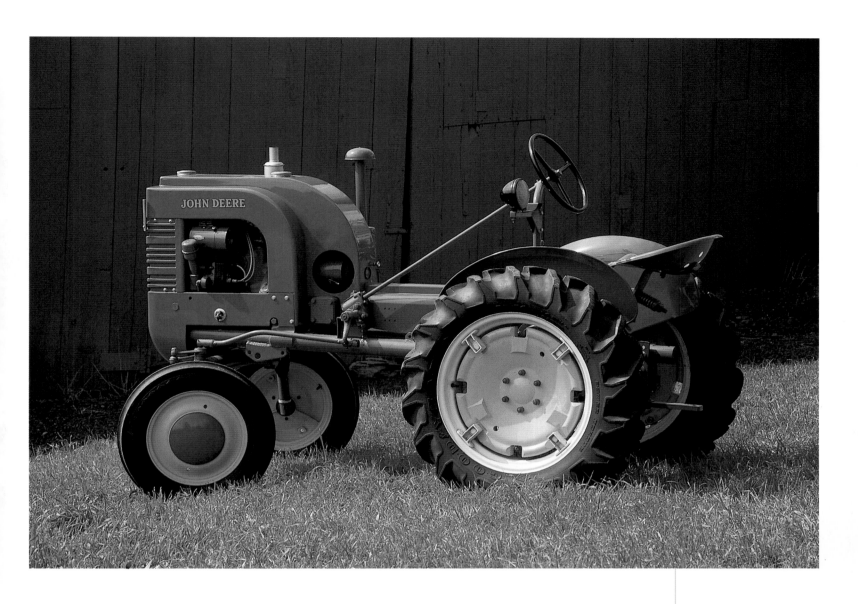

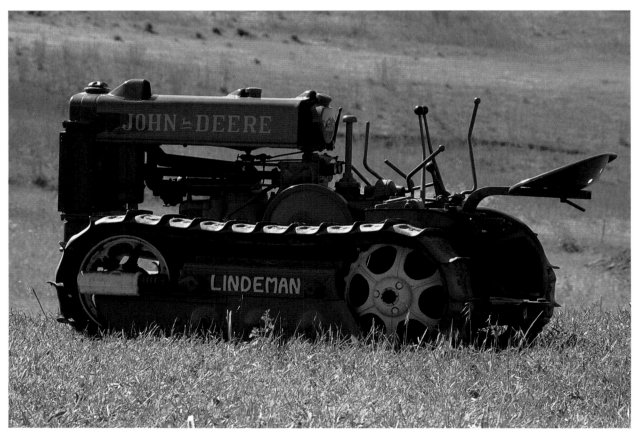

ABOVE: *The John Deere Model L is a great favorite of collectors. With an 8-horsepower motor, the little L was the perfect size for nurserymen and other small agricultural operations. Built between 1937 and 1946, the Model L could almost fit into your back pocket.*

LEFT: *The Lindeman tractor is really a converted John Deere Model B that an equipment dealer created in the late 1930s. The conversion was the brainchild of former Cletrac dealer Jesse Lindeman, who paired a Deere body with a set of Best tracks. Even Deere liked the idea.*

## Ford-Ferguson: The Model 9N Saves the Day

In addition to the Oliver, one other tremendous innovation in tractor design appeared in the 1930s. Arriving late in the decade (1939), it would move the industry forward by a quantum leap. This innovation was the three-point hitch and the hydraulic system, developed by Harry Ferguson for use on the Ford tractors.

Henry Ford, as we recall, brought out the Fordson tractor in 1916, during World War I, and shipped six thousand tractors to Europe to help rebuild the continent after the war. But although the Fordson was a cheap tractor, and nearly 750,000 Fordson tractors were built in the decade or so that it was produced, it was not admired or greatly respected. Its most attractive feature was its low price, not its engineering or utility.

Other tractor builders produced a full line of plows, planters, cultivators, seeders, and the service to go with them, but Fordson owners soon found that Ford sold only tractors, not implements. While you could hitch any sort of implement to the back of the Fordson and usually get the job done, it soon became clear that having a well-designed set of tools—ones that fit the specifications of the particular tractor—was very important.

Safety was also important, and, here again, the Fordson had problems. It quickly earned a reputation for flipping over backward if the farmer encountered a snag. There was no way to cut the Fordson motor fast enough to keep the tractor from digging in its rear wheels and rearing up, dumping the driver and pinning him under the machine.

The Fordson stopped being profitable in 1926, after the enormously popular Farmall was introduced, and by 1928 the Fordson had reached the end of its run. Although Henry Ford was making some efforts to improve his tractor, a series of corporate events, along with the Depression, shut down American production of the Fordson tractor, although it continued to be built in Ireland for the European market.

Harry Ferguson, a tough and brilliant inventor, first developed a system of draft control that would change the fortunes of Ford's tractor. Born in Ireland in 1884, Ferguson was a natural mechanic. While still a teen, he was repairing and selling motorcycles and autos. By 1909, he had built his own airplane in which he made the first recorded

*BELOW: **Although the Fordson sold widely in Europe as well as the United States, the Fordson simply lagged behind competing tractors. Squat and clunky, the machine, like this 1937 model, could not compete with the Farmall and the agile rowcrop tractors.***

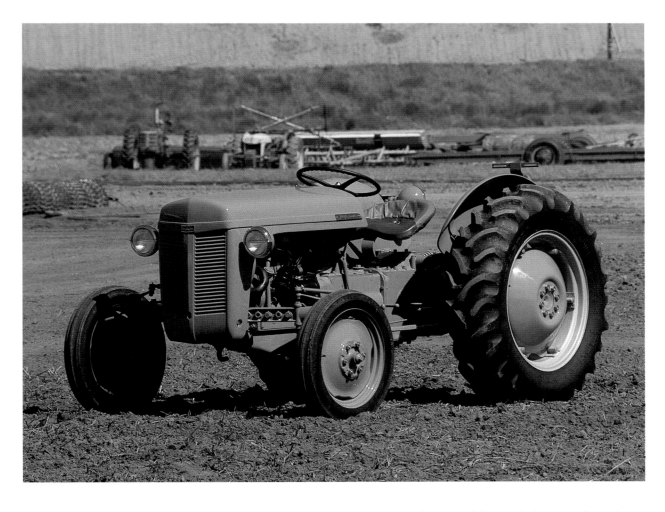

flight in Ireland. Ferguson became interested in the economic conditions of the Irish farmer, observing that a low-cost tractor with a reliable plow would improve the Irish economy.

A problem common to all tractors was controlling the depth of the plow blade, keeping the furrows at a uniform depth as the tractor rolled along. Harry Ferguson had first developed his draft control system before 1916, attaching it to a tractor known as the Eros. But the Eros company disappeared, due in large part to the introduction of the cheap Fordson.

As the years went by, Ferguson continued to develop farm machinery. He refined and improved the Ferguson system and eventually introduced an improved draft control system that impressed Ford managers. Demonstrated in 1938, the new mechanism was operated with hydraulics, powered by the tractor's engine. In addition to draft control, the driver could now raise and lower the plows and other implements just by operating a single lever, without leaving his seat. It was also now possible for the farmer to attach or remove a wide range of equipment in about a minute. The Ford Company immediately began preliminary production of the tractor that would be introduced in 1939, the Model 9N. It would be known as the Ford-Ferguson, a Ford tractor with the Ferguson system.

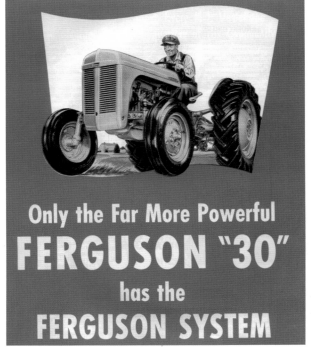

Only the Far More Powerful
**FERGUSON "30"**
has the
**FERGUSON SYSTEM**

# A FEW TRACTOR TERMS

*Hanging around tractor shows will add a few new words to your vocabulary. Here are a few of the basics:*

**Big Red**—Farmall, or International Harvester, the largest competition to the Green Machine (John Deere, see below).

**Crawler**—A tractor that rolls on steel treads rather than wheels. Caterpillar and Cletrac are two brands of early crawlers.

**Distillate**—The early type of petrolem fuel that was used for tractors. Like kerosene, it was in widespread use for tractors until the mid-1930s, when the Oliver 70 was introduced.

**Green Machine**—John Deere. John Deere tractor enthusiasts are the largest group of tractor collectors around. Be polite.

**Horse Farming**—Farming with horses rather than with tractors. This is not to be confused with "horse raising," which refers to breeding and showing horses for profit.

**Johnny Popper**—A John Deere, two-cylinder tractor, that makes the characteristic pop-pop sound.

**Lesser-known Classic**—A group of tractors that were widely respected in their day and well known within their own region but are just beginning to be appreciated by collectors. The Silver King is an example.

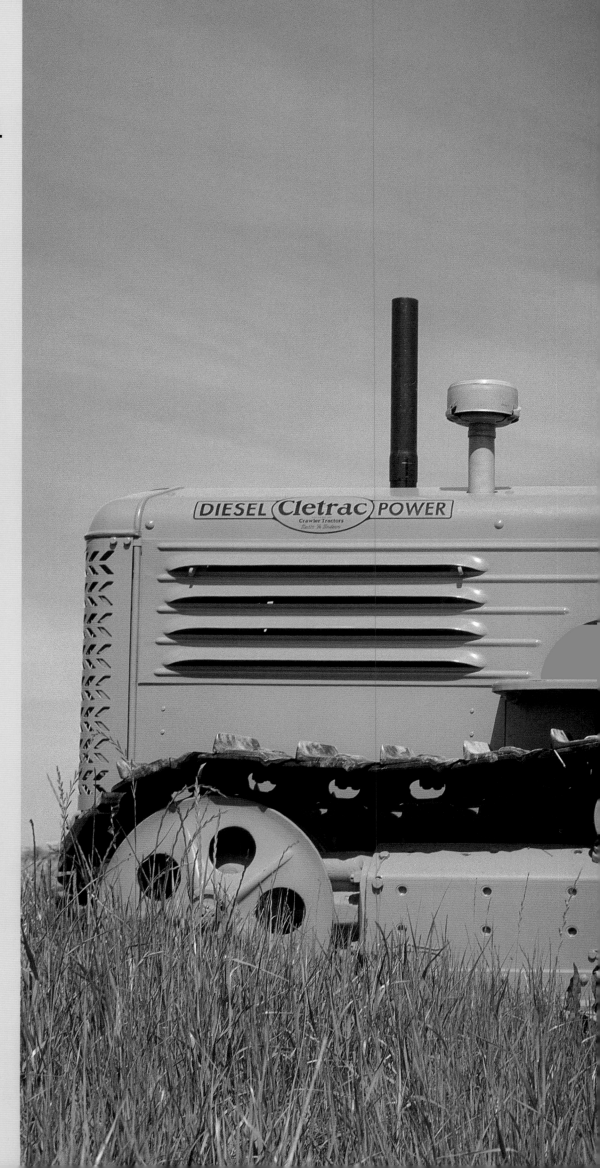

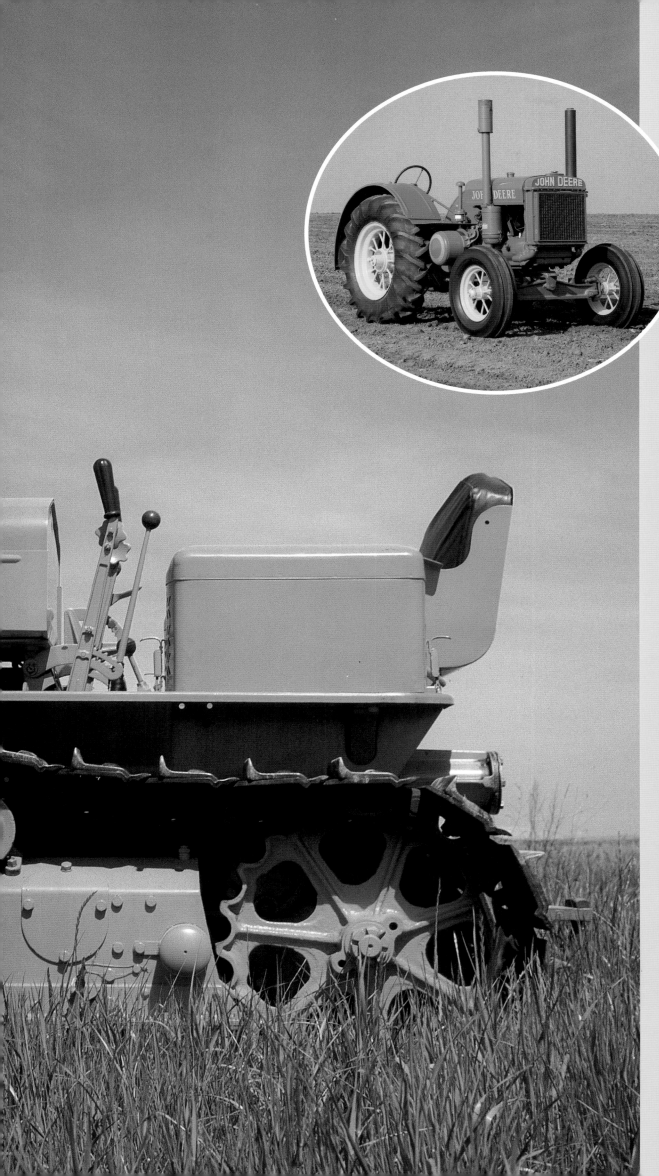

**Minnie-Mo**—The shorthand term for the Minneapolis-Moline Company, builder of a very solid and reliable tractor.

**On Steel**—Tractors with large steel wheels rather than rubber tires. Usually fitted with cleats or lugs, these wheels offer better traction in the field but cannot be driven on roads.

**Rollag**—The annual show in Rollag, Minnesota, for steam tractor enthusiasts. Harley riders go to Sturgis, but real iron men go to Rollag.

**Tractor Pull**—An event, frequently held at county and state fairs, where tractors compete to pull heavy loads.

**Tulare**—A county in the Central Valley of California that hosts one of the biggest displays of vintage tractors in the country.

*LEFT:* **Crawlers, like this Cletrac, are sometimes overlooked by the casual observer, but this type of tractor has an important place in agricultural history.**

*INSET:* **Known as the Green Machine, or Johnny Popper, John Deere tractors receive tremendous loyalty from their owners.**

The economy was beginning to recover by 1939, and the new Ford 9N with its power lift sold ten thousand units by the end of the year. In addition to the system that allowed implements to be attached quickly, Ford introduced a system of linkages on the wheels and axles that enabled the farmer to widen the width of the tractor tread easily. This made the tractor quickly adaptable for various types of crops, all grown with different spacing between the rows.

Beyond that, the Ford-Ferguson tractor was cheap. The introductory price was only $585.00, about half the price of machines from other builders. It did not include a starter or rubber tires or many of the other features already offered as standard on the Oliver or the Farmall, but it seemed to be a good, practical, and inexpensive machine for the average farmer. Ford would sell nearly 100,000 9N tractors before the model was discontinued during the middle of World War II. It was replaced in 1942 with Ford's Model 2N, a machine with a few more amenities, such as a starter.

## The U-DLX: A Machine Ahead of Its Time

BELOW: *The most critical piece of the tractor to many collectors, the serial number stamped on the maker's plate pinpoints the year of manufacture.*

Another highly styled vehicle that appeared in the late 1930s was the Minneapolis-Moline Company's U-DLX "Comfortractor." With its completely enclosed cab, this tractor looked more like the family sedan than a farm workhorse. The entire machine was covered with curved and formed sheet metal, presenting an aerodynamic appearance. It was actually an extremely practical machine for the Minnesota and Wisconsin area, or any other place with freezing temperatures. But farmers were just not ready for such a large change from the conventional tractors they were used to seeing.

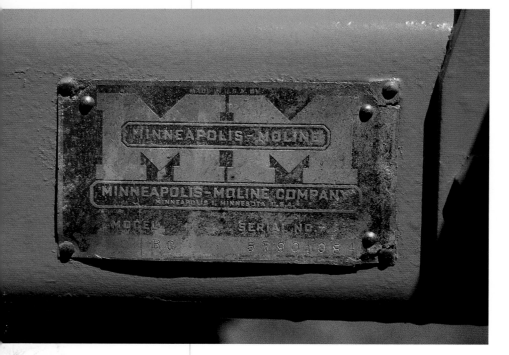

The U-DLX had windshield wipers, a defroster, and a heater. It was just the machine to drive on those January mornings when someone has to haul hay to the cattle in the far pasture or chop ice on the pond. It was a widely publicized tractor that received a great deal of media attention, but sales were slow.

Perhaps due to timing or perhaps due to price, the machine was just not popular with farmers. Introduced at the end of the Depression and just at the beginning of World War II, fewer than 150 machines were built between 1938 and 1941. The U-DLX cost more than two thousand dollars apiece, a heftier price than a comparable Deere or Farmall. Today, however, because of its rarity and its remarkable styling, the U-DLX has come into its own and is highly prized by collectors.

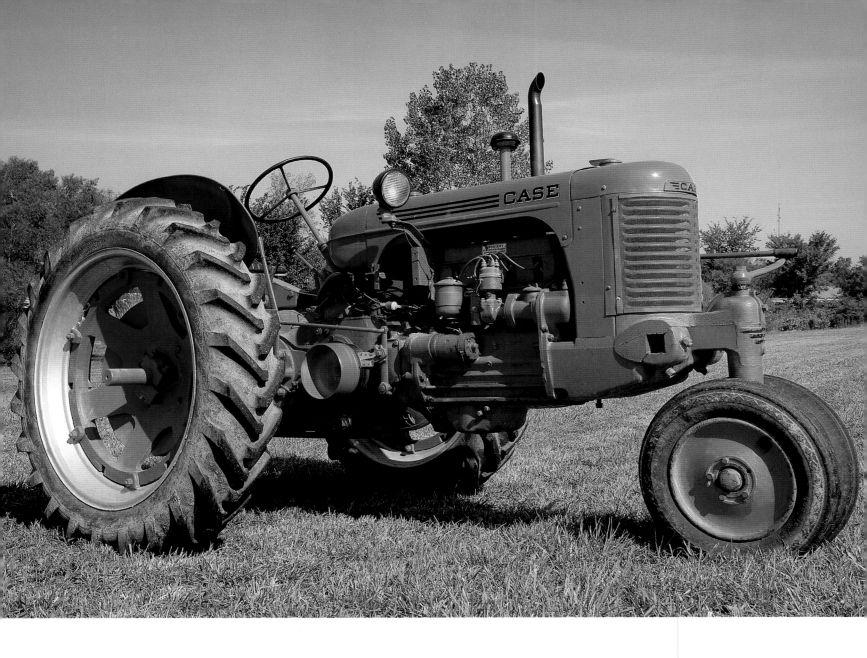

## A New Color for Case

Like the other builders, Case was hit hard during the Depression. Tractor production at the firm peaked at more than sixteen thousand units in 1930. Just three years later, only 574 units were sold all year. But corporate conservatism saved the company, and Case found that it did not have to make the drastic cuts in staffing that decimated many of its competitors. Case entered the Depression with a sizable cash cushion and was able to hang on.

Business was a little better in 1934 and 1935, although a drought continued to plague farm production. Still, Case made plans to update its product line. It had already introduced its own version of the Ferguson system in 1935 with a Case "motor lift" system designed to raise implements, and styling changes were in the works when the new models were introduced, but it would be a few years before the look of the entire product line changed.

A new paint job was the first priority, but a glance at the competition revealed that all the good colors were taken: green, red, orange, yellow—Deere, Farmall, and other builders had made them their own. The Case marketing department settled for something they called Flambeau Red, a red-orange that became the signature color for Case.

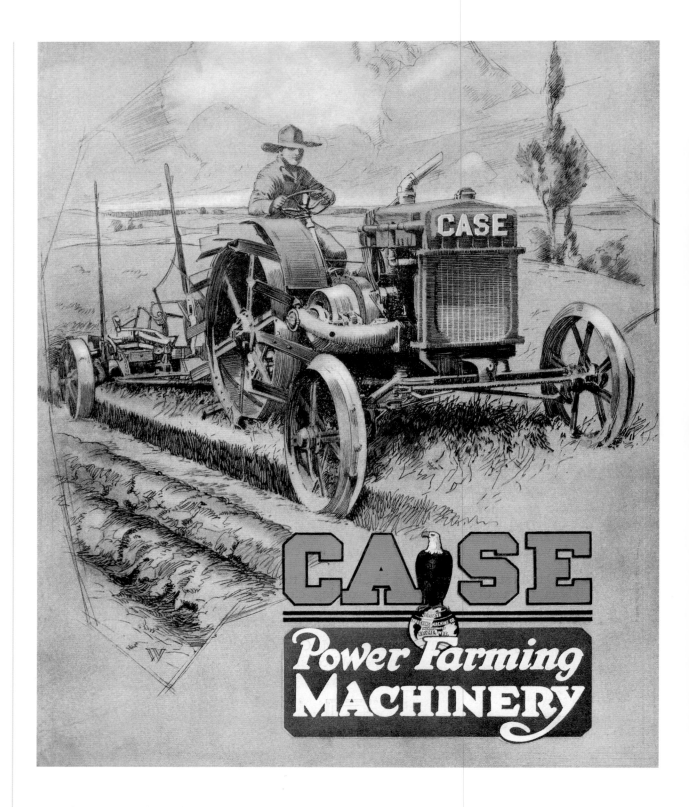

RIGHT: *The jaunty exhaust pipe identifies this tractor as a cross-motor, a series of machines introduced around 1920. The engine is mounted sideways, and thus provides extraordinary efficiency.*

The Case machine that finally met the competition head on was the Model D, brought out in 1939. This was the model that introduced Flambeau Red, and it had adjustable wheels, a power lift system for implements, and something called "eagle eye" visibility, allowing drivers a much better view of their work.

The Depression and the war years were as tough for tractor builders as they were for so many businesses. Many of the smaller manufacturers disappeared altogether, leaving just a handful: Allis and Oliver, Minnie-Mo and Massey-Ferguson, McCormick, Deere, and Case. Less than a dozen tractor builders, large and small, were still around after the war. Competition and innovation would continue to whittle away the ranks.

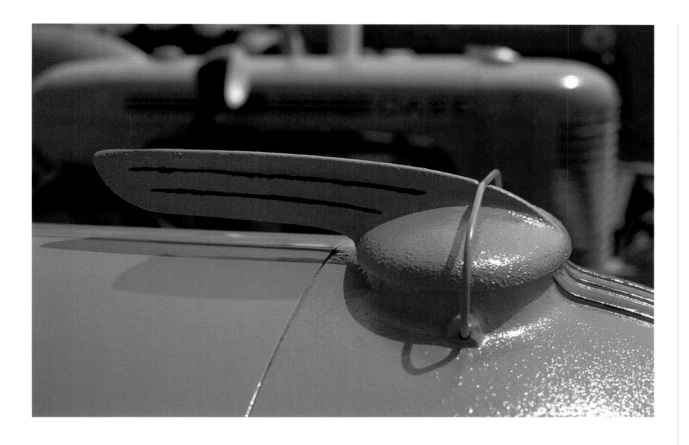

*LEFT: Case redesigned its Model L right down to the gas cap. Since it was wartime, the gas cap is somewhat restrained, but it still manages to convey the overall aerodynamic feel of the new styling.*

*BELOW: Case collectors say they like the variations between the different Case models. In front is a 1935 Rowcrop (Model RC) and in back is a Model L, which first came out in 1929. Both are owned by Dale Hartley.*

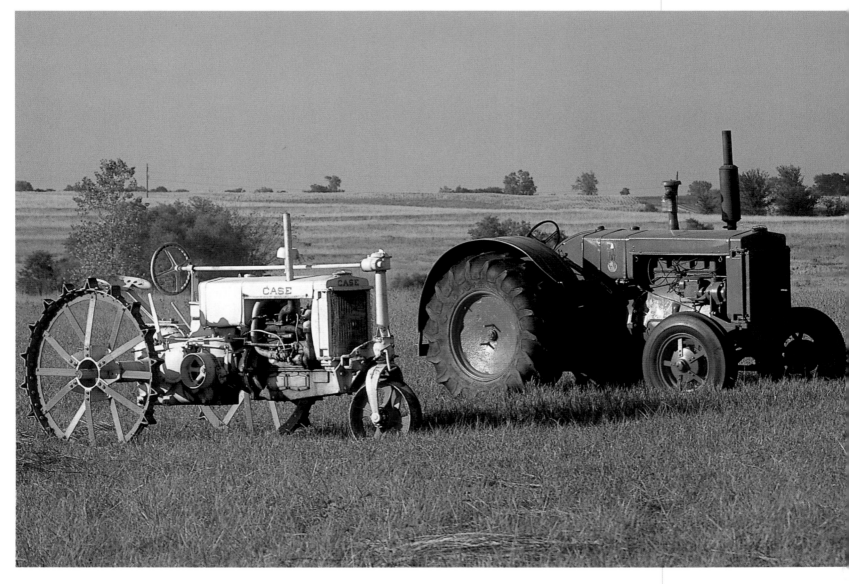

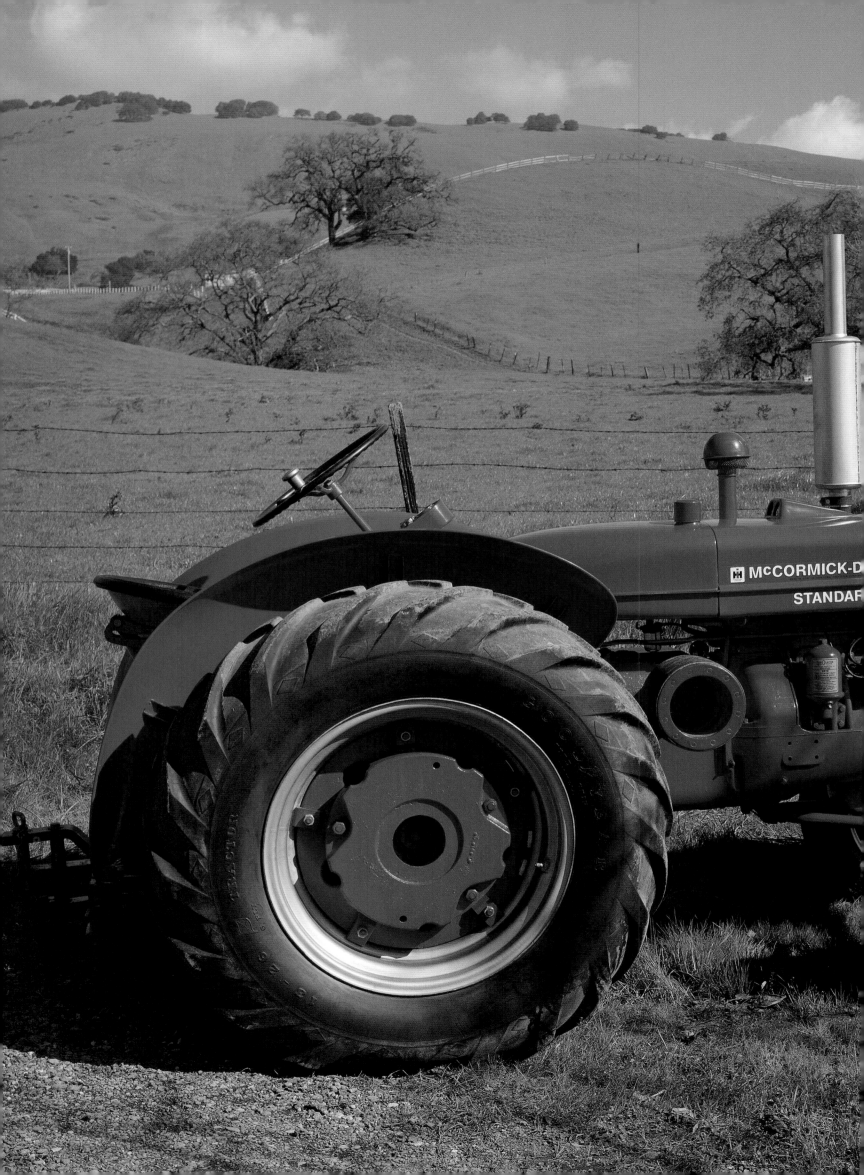

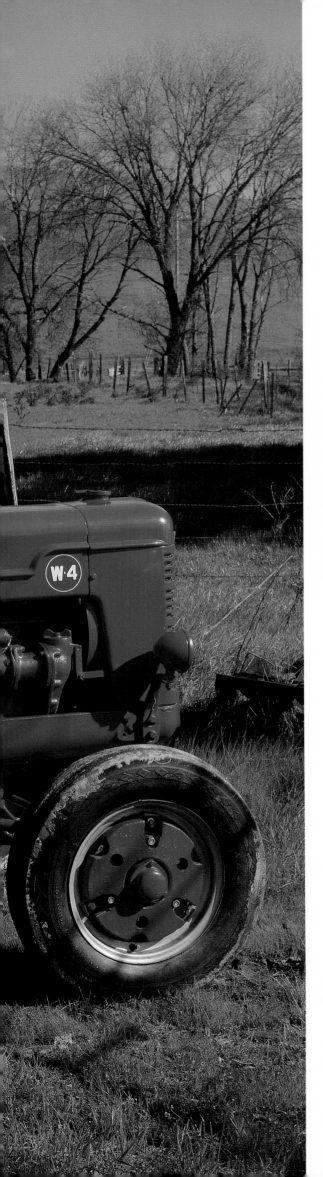

# TRACTORS MEET THE FUTURE

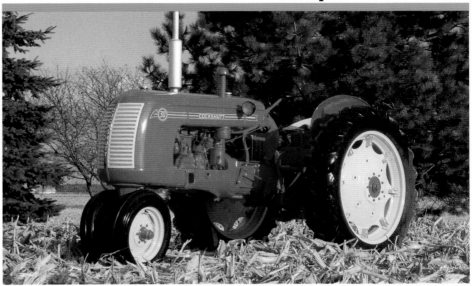

## Chapter Four

**T**he end of the war brought enormous changes to all walks of American life. Farming changed dramatically, too, thanks to some lessons learned during those tough years. First of all, materials that had been in scarce supply during World War II, like steel and rubber, were now available to build better tractors.

Second, during wartime, the country had learned to be a lot more efficient in many areas, including farming. Lines from the song written about World War I soldiers were still true thirty years later: it was hard to keep them down on the farm after they had seen "Paree." Farmers were going to need all the mechanical help they could get to replace the farm boy who had taken a city job.

*LEFT: **Beautiful yet extremely efficient, the W-4 came out in 1940 to help with the war effort. It remains an all-time favorite because of its rugged construction and looks.***

*ABOVE: **The Cockshutt is a regional favorite, from Ontario, Canada. This model was introduced in 1947 and is sure to remain popular with collectors due to its beautiful styling.***

The improving economy released pent-up demand for consumer products. For nearly fifteen years, the Depression and then the war had prevented the average consumer from replacing old and worn-out equipment. Suddenly, manufacturers couldn't turn out new products fast enough—new houses, new cars, new refrigerators, and, of course, new tractors.

Tractors built after the war benefited from the improved engineering and production methods learned during those years. Now tractors could be built with diesel engines, better hydraulics, and all sorts of options that became standard equipment, such as electric starters and headlights.

Tractor builders had always kept an eye on the automobile market, watching for trends that might have an impact on the tractor buyer. During the early 1950s, automatic transmissions were an immediate hit when they were introduced on most major automobiles. Tractor builders quickly followed suit, and automatic transmissions would become the last major innovation before the Golden Age of tractors came to a close at the end of the decade.

## Ford versus Ferguson

The Ferguson hydraulic hitch system allowed the farmer to be extremely efficient and helped make the Ford a leader in tractor engineering. The Ferguson lift was greatly envied by other tractor builders, who had now developed a similar device of their own but were restrained from production by patent law. In 1938, Ford and Ferguson had decided to collaborate and had sealed their partnership with just a handshake.

During the war years, Ford sold a cheap, stripped-down tractor that met wartime restrictions. The Ford 2N came without a starter, generator, or rubber tires. Presumably, farmers could scrounge these essentials from older machines. But after the end of the war, some dramatic changes occurred at the Ford Motor Company that had a profound impact on both the Ford Motor Company and the tractor industry as a whole.

The first change was the death of Henry Ford himself. When he died in 1945, at age eighty, his empire was left under the leadership of his dynamic grandson, twenty-eight-year-old Henry Ford II. The second major change for Ford tractors was the

BELOW: *The Ford Motor Company celebrated its fiftieth anniversary in 1953. Ignoring the historical reality that Ford and Fordson had been two completely separate companies, tractors built after 1953 all feature the anniversary logo on their nose. The reconciliation was good for business.*

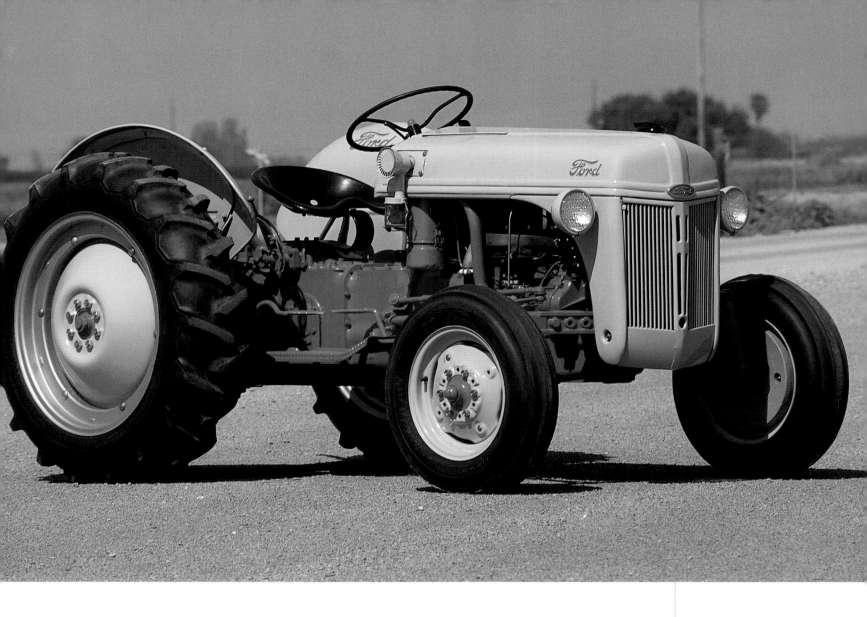

introduction of their first newly designed postwar tractor, one with all the features and improvements the farmer now expected. The new Ford 8N was ready for market in 1948.

Finally, Henry Ford II decided to end Ford's business relationship with Harry Ferguson. For more than a decade, Ford tractors had been sold and serviced by a Ferguson dealership network. In addition, Ford had paid Ferguson a royalty for using the Ferguson hitch system. Now this would all end. Ford would not pay the royalty, secured only by his grandfather's famous "handshake agreement," but Ford would continue to use Ferguson's hitch. Lawsuits ensued.

The Ford and Ferguson litigation had a tremendous impact on the entire tractor industry. Other manufacturers had carefully copied the Ferguson system, making changes and refinements that would cleverly skirt the existing patents. Now they were prevented from selling their own versions of the Ferguson system by the patent review that was wending its way through the courts.

The lawsuit was finally settled in 1952, and Ferguson took out full-page ads in the newspapers. He had sued for $251 million and received a little more than nine million dollars. The other tractor builders heaved a sigh of relief. The early Ferguson patents had now lapsed. Soon tractors from every major builder would include a variation of the ingenious Ferguson hitch.

*ABOVE: **Young Henry Ford II refused to pay inventor Harry Ferguson a royalty for the lift system used by the new Ford 8N. The resulting litigation brought some tremendous changes to the tractor industry. Then Ferguson's patents expired, allowing copycat designers an opportunity to imitate Ferguson's brilliant engineering.***

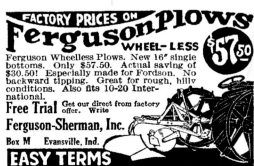

FACTORY PRICES ON
**Ferguson Plows**
WHEEL-LESS $57.50

Ferguson Wheelless Plows. New 16" single bottoms. Only $57.50. Actual saving of $30.50! Especially made for Fordson. No backward tipping. Great for rough, hilly conditions. Also fits 10-20 International.

**Free Trial** Get our direct from factory offer. Write

**Ferguson-Sherman, Inc.**
Box M    Evansville, Ind.
**EASY TERMS**

## "Small" Innovations from International Harvester

The most exciting offering to come from International Harvester just after World War II was the Farmall Cub. It weighed only about fifteen hundred pounds, less than half of conventional tractors, and it came with a variety of attachments. The Cub was just the machine for nurseries, vegetable growers, landscape contractors, and farmers with only a few acres.

Like its big brother, the Farmall Model A, the little machine came with *cultivision*, the offset steering system. It also had an electric starter, headlights, and seven or eight implements scaled specifically for a smaller tractor. A power takeoff was available, as was a hydraulic system for raising and lowering all those terrific little accessories. It looked so much like the Farmall Model A that many collectors still have trouble telling them apart from a distance.

The Cub was good competition for John Deere's Model L, the "Little," which first appeared a decade earlier in 1938. With its many updates, the Cub would remain in the International catalog until the 1960s. (Nowadays, it's a great favorite among collectors with limited space.)

But the marketplace was changing, propelled by Henry Ford and his 9N. After the war, Deere was selling about twenty-five thousand tractors a year to the small farms with one hundred acres or fewer. This figure included sales of the four smaller Deere models: the Model B, Models L and LA, and the H. In comparison, Ford was selling more than forty thousand units of the 9N, its only tractor, to the same customers.

Smart tractor builders took another look at Ford's offering. John Deere dropped its little tractors in favor of a Model M, dubbed a "utility" tractor. And International began to promote a Ford look-alike, the four-wheel McCormick-Deering, along with its tricycle-style Farmall.

International Harvester would remain competitive, bringing out a wide range of tractors with all the options the market demanded. Diesel engines were now available on many models, as was a power system that allowed quick and easy attachment of accessories. The Farmall models for the 1950s were numbered: Models 100, 200, and 300. With their increased performance and rounded grille, they form a beautiful package, the best of both worlds in tractor design. These machines combine performance and style.

After the 1960s, the engineering options on tractors began to escalate. Four-wheel drive, power steering, roll-bars, and enclosed cabs would all begin to make their appearance. But tractors also began to take on a squared, boxy appearance that does not have as much eye appeal as the earlier machines. Automobiles were getting fins and a lot of chrome, but tractors were not getting the glamour treatment at all.

BELOW: *International Harvester always kept an eye on the marketplace and soon realized that the small farmer needed specialized equipment too.*

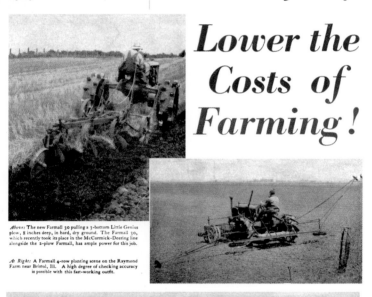

*Above:* The new Farmall 30 pulling a 3-bottom Little Genius plow, 8 inches deep, in hard, dry ground. The Farmall 30, which recently took its place in the McCormick-Deering line alongside the 2-plow Farmall, has ample power for this job.

*At Right:* A Farmall 4-row planting scene on the Raymond Farm near Bristol, Ill. A high degree of checking accuracy is possible with this fast-working outfit.

**McCORMICK-DEERING TRACTORS**
15-30 »» 2-PLOW FARMALL »« 3-PLOW FARMALL «« 10-20

OPPOSITE: *International Harvester brought out tractors in both their Farmall and the McCormick-Deering Standard lines with many additional comfort and safety features. They paid special attention to improving engine performance. International Harvester had a notable edge over the two-cylinder John Deere tractors.*

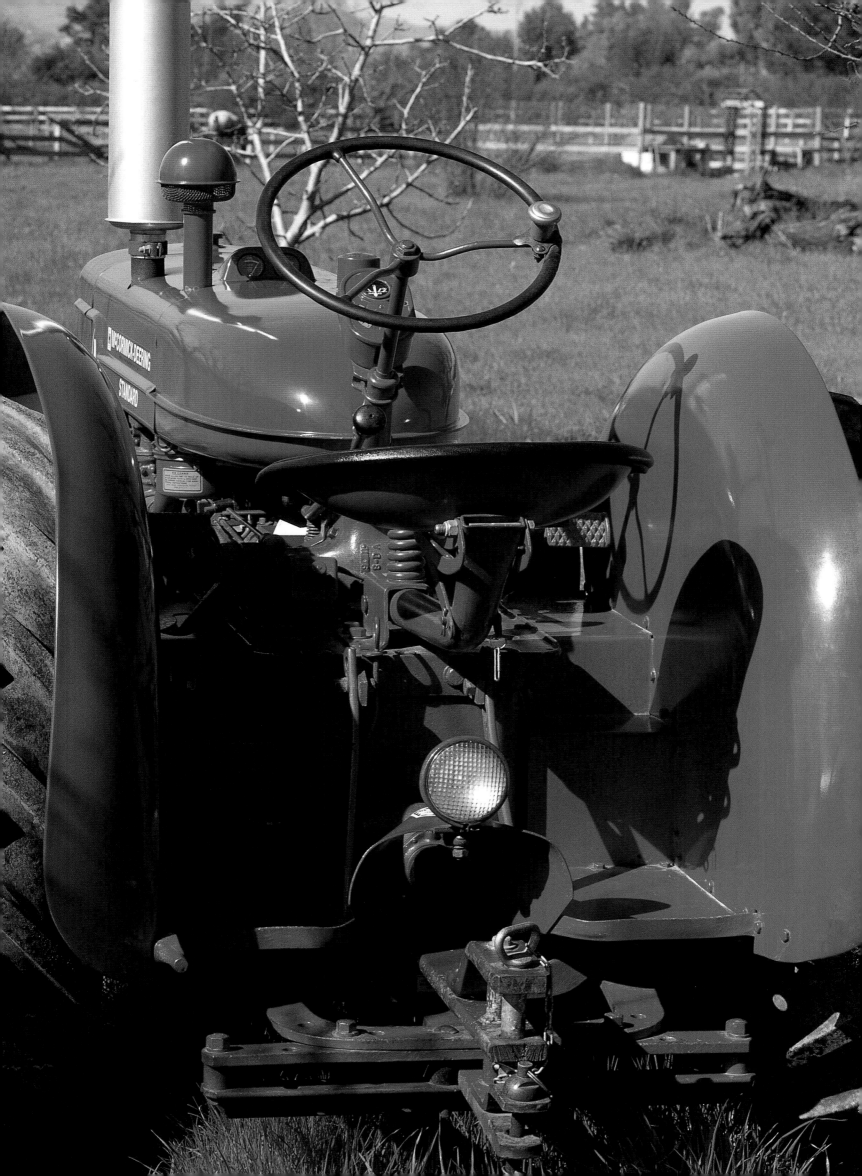

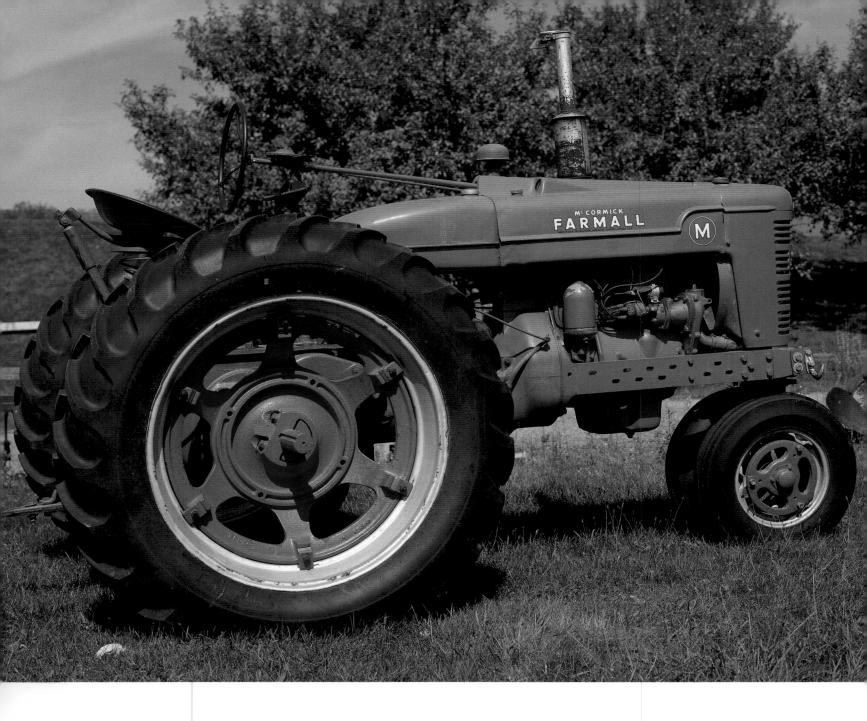

*ABOVE: The Farmall M was introduced in 1939 but remained in production until the early 1950s. More than a quarter of a million tractors were sold, a solid testimonial to its usefulness and durability.*

## Diesel Comes into Its Own

Sometimes a new star just has to sit backstage, waiting for the leading lady to break a leg. Diesel engines had been around for nearly fifty years, proving their value by providing power to locomotives and ships. Smaller diesel engines, first used in earthmoving equipment in the 1920s, had been developed and refined. The Caterpillar Company had used diesel engines for decades.

But fuel availability and pricing had limited diesels to large-scale commercial uses. During the Depression, many states with large railroad operations decided to tax diesel fuel, hoping to squeeze some additional revenue into their pockets. The kerosene derivatives used by tractors remained a lot more desirable.

Diesel was just waiting for the right opportunity to perform, though. In 1937, International Harvester introduced a little diesel-powered crawler called the TracTractor. Designed to compete with Caterpillar, the machine proved to be very cheap to operate. Following this success, IH then introduced a tractor with a diesel engine, offering diesel as an option on the 1941 Farmall "Mighty" M.

While the new engine cost fifty percent more than a conventional engine, fuel savings quickly offset the expense.

Other builders waited until after the war to add a diesel-powered tractor to their product line. John Deere introduced tractors with both a hydraulic lift system and a diesel engine to its catalog in 1949. Now Deere could compete successfully with Ford and International Harvester.

## Case Keeps Pace

Case offered its version of the hydraulic lift in 1949, calling it the Eagle Hitch. During the war years, Case had made many small improvements to its tractors, but by the early 1950s it was ready for a dramatic change. In 1953, the company brought out the Case 300. "Daring, Dazzling and Dynamic" blared the headlines.

Three sizes were offered—Models 300, 400, and 500. Finally, the loyal Case customer had a tremendous selection. Case 300 came with hydraulics, two different transmissions, and a choice of four fuel options: diesel, gasoline, LPG fuel, or distillate. Buyers could opt for a four-, eight-, or twelve-speed transmission. And there were six versions: a general-purpose tractor as well as orchard, high-clearance, row crop, industrial, and utility models. Whew! In addition, Case brought out its "Case-o-matic" drive in 1957 in response to the raging success of the automatic transmission in the automobile market.

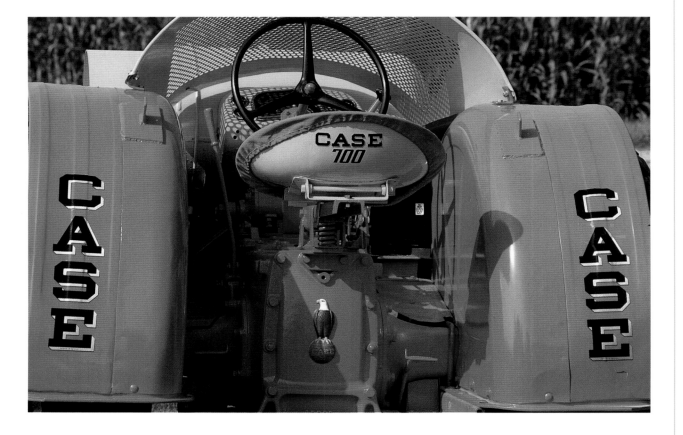

*LEFT: **Old Abe, the famous Case eagle, gets a ride on this new Case orchard tractor, the Case 700. The two-toned paint scheme was introduced in 1955 along with an automatic transmission and many other improvements. This machine belongs in the Case orchard tractor collection of JR Gyger.***

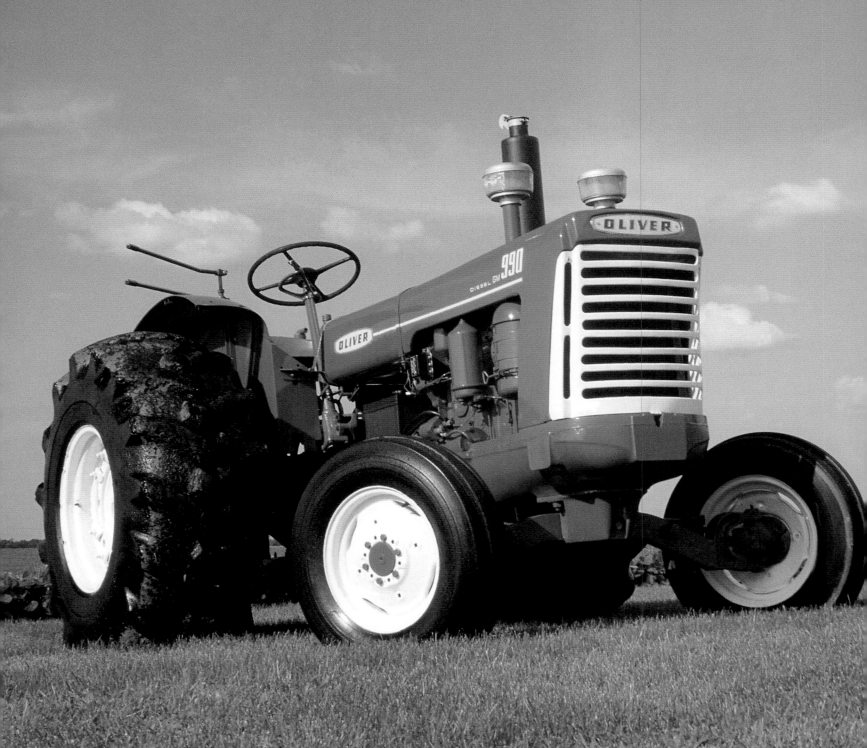

# Farewell to Oliver

While Oliver had waited out the war with its existing models, after the war the company was quick to produce a diesel, first offering it as an option in 1947. Oliver also understood the reasons behind the overwhelming popularity of the Ford: farmers wanted a small, economical utility tractor with a three-point hitch. In response, Oliver soon manufactured and marketed Model 55, a tractor that looked and handled like a Ford. It was also one of the first tractors on the market with a twelve-volt electrical system. For the first time, tractors offered the same reliable systems found on cars.

Oliver had some terrific design ideas, but was not always able to bring them to the marketplace. The company could not keep up with larger manufacturers that had more money. The firm seemed to lose its edge in the 1950s: its most memorable machine from that decade was the Super 44, a tractor reminiscent of a grasshopper because the steering assembly protruded through the front of the grille and the tie-rods overhung the front of the frame. Its strange design was certainly not typical of the extraordinary innovation that had been an Oliver hallmark. The Super 44 was built in Battle Creek, Michigan, rather than at the Charles City plant. It broke with tradition in another way, offering an offset seat and steering similar to the *Cultivision* concept trademarked by International Harvester a generation earlier.

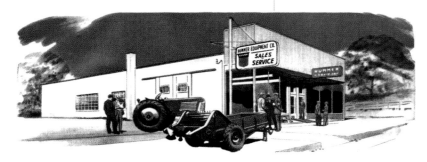

**"OLIVER'S Progress has paid off for us"**

It was a small machine, competing with the Ford, and it came with hydraulics as well as all the other bells and whistles that the competition was offering. But, overall, the little machine was odd looking and poorly designed, a far cry from the beautiful Oliver 70 that had been an industry leader in its time.

Design notes from the Oliver files reveal a list of dazzling innovations. The engineers' wish list included an enclosed, all-weather cab with heating, air conditioning, tinted glass, and a comfortable, completely adjustable seat, as well as a radio, a cigarette lighter, and an ashtray. Additional instrumentation would include a tachometer, a gauge to record the number of hours of operation, and an automatic barn door opener. Safety features were on the list, too, making every work platform skidproof, and adding seatbelts and a roll-bar for head protection.

These innovations, visionary at the time, are today all regular features on most tractors. Wishful thinking does not sell tractors, though, and the extraordinary Oliver Company would soon disappear. In 1960, it celebrated the twenty-fifth anniversary of its introduction of the "Most Beautiful Tractor Ever Built." Later that year it was gone, swallowed up by the White Motor Company of Cleveland. In need of cash to modernize its manufacturing plant, it had fallen prey to a larger competitor with more money.

*FOLLOWING PAGES: The John Deere Model L, sometimes called the "Little," was introduced in 1938 for nurserymen and other growers with small acreage. It is now one of the most popular tractors for collectors.*

*BELOW: Hart-Parr Oliver pioneered the concept of customer service, as this ad serves to remind us.*

*OPPOSITE: In general, the 1960s were sad times for tractor design. Just compare this machine to the one following. The smooth aerodynamic lines were abandoned in favor of the boxy, squared off appearance that was common on many popular motor cars. Oliver also abandoned its traditional paint scheme in favor of light green and white. It was the beginning of the end.*

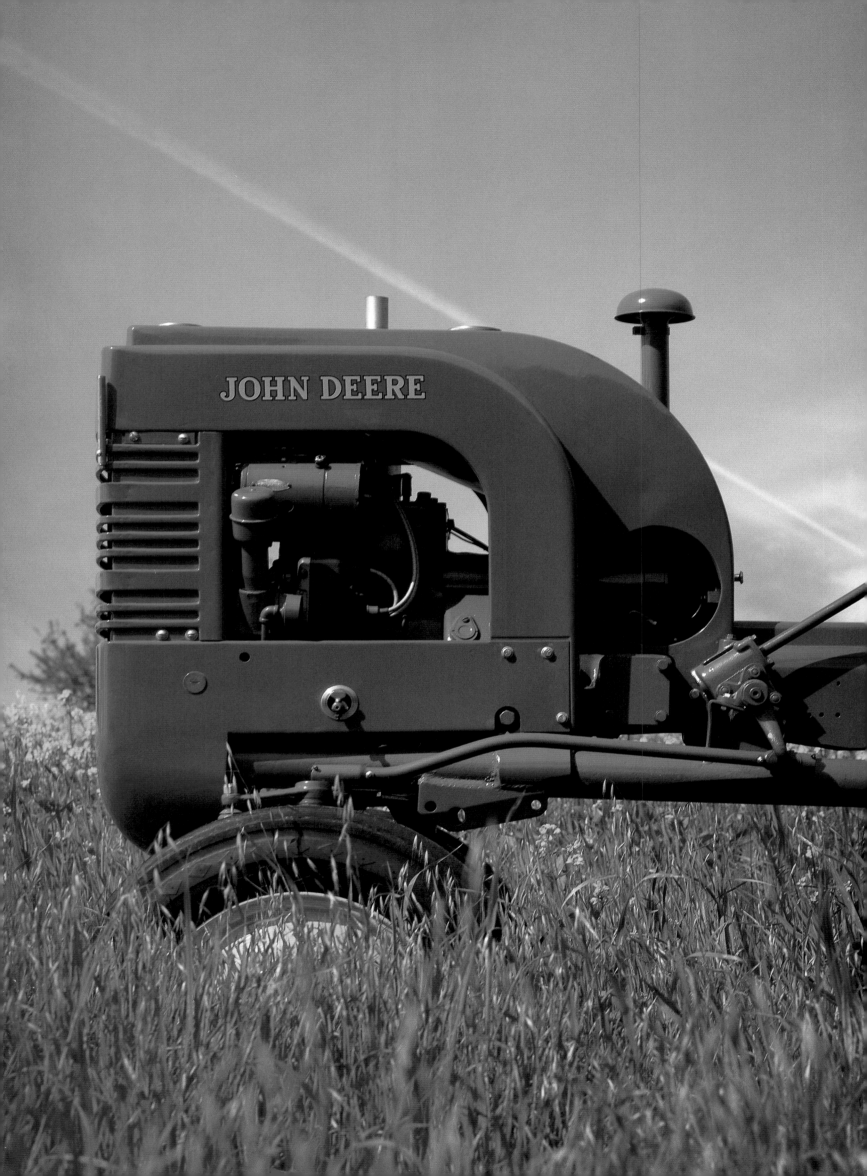

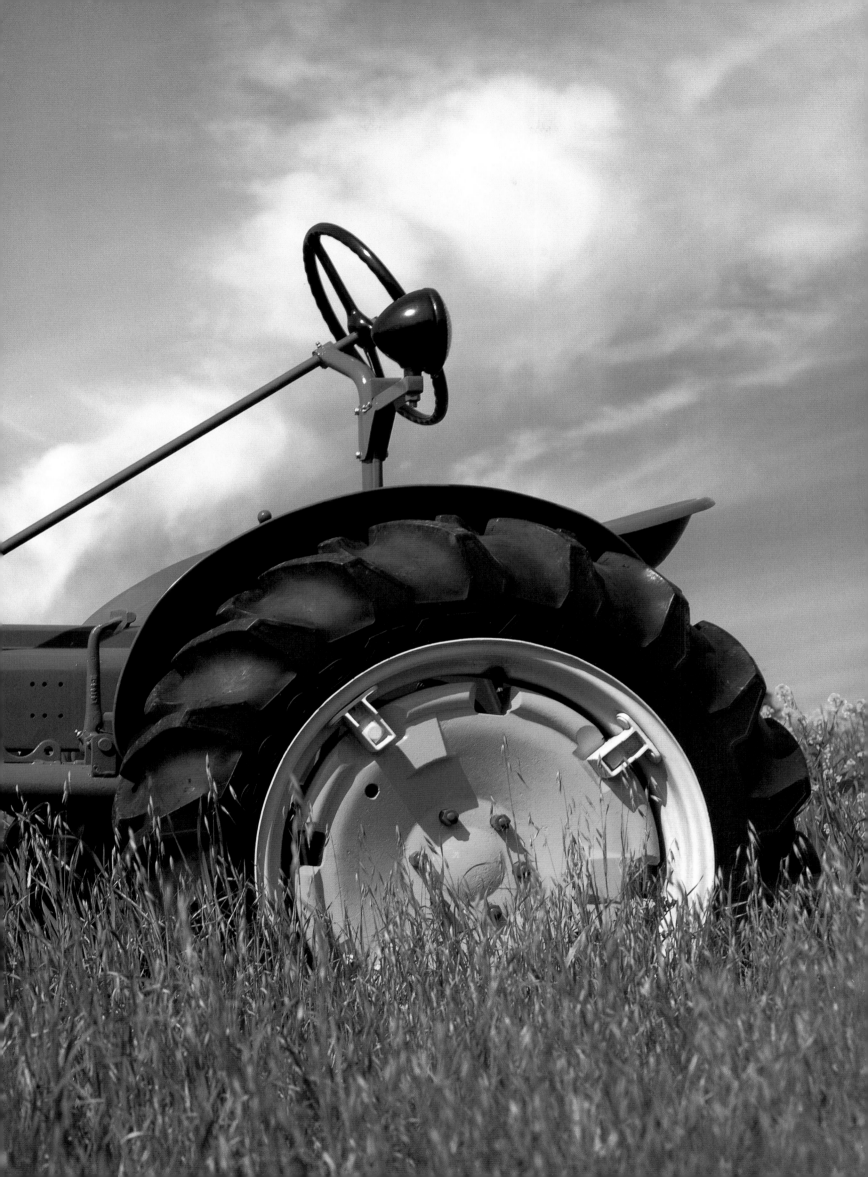

*BELOW: **This John Deere 2355 orchard tractor, introduced after 1960, illustrates the current direction of Deere styling. Deere retained its easily recognizable signature green hue. Perhaps this machine will qualify as a future collectible, but the old pop-pop sound is gone forever.***

## Nothing Runs Like a Deere

Tractor builders had a watershed year in 1949. Although International Harvester was the market leader, the postwar years would see the steady growth of the John Deere Company and its remarkable dominance in the tractor market. Deere's first significant postwar offering was the Model M, a smallish, 18-horsepower tractor with an electric starter and the "Touch-O-Matic" hydraulic control system. The Model M was built to compete directly with the Ford.

In addition, Deere upgraded its older tractor models, adding lights, electric starters, and high-compression engines. It also began to offer a diesel engine and brought out a diesel tractor, the Model R. Deere now felt it could compete successfully with Ford and International Harvester.

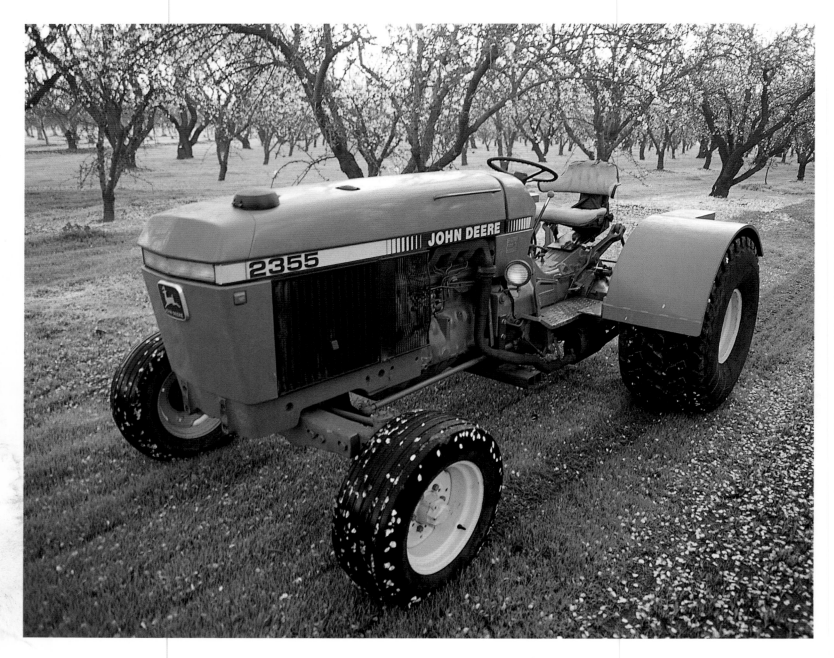

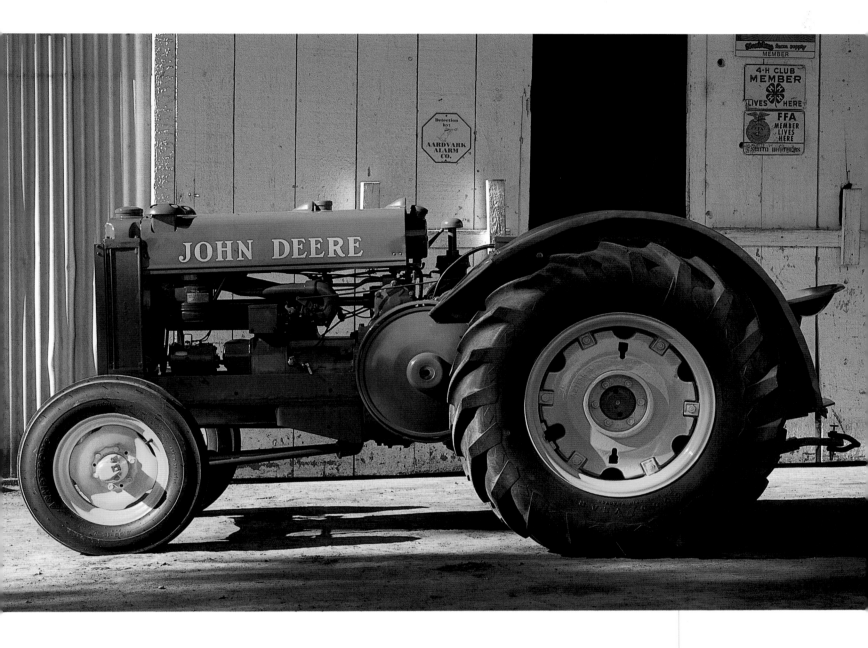

The Deere product line received a complete overhaul in the 1950s, enabling the company to market a full range of sizes and all the options that other tractor builders were selling. In 1954, Deere became the first manufacturer to offer factory-installed power steering on a tractor. Deere machines now came with Custom Power-Trol (Deere's answer to the Ferguson system) and with a comfortable seat known as the Float-Ride. But despite the many features and options that John Deere offered, one critical element was still missing: a four-cylinder engine.

For nearly forty years, John Deere had been known for its green machine, the Johnny Popper, that solid little tractor with its distinctive "pop-pop" sound. In the modern world, with larger tractors and a bigger workload, the little two-cylinder engine had reached the upper limit of its capability. The Johnny Popper was retired in 1960.

*ABOVE:* **The early John Deere models, such as this terrific Model AO with its offset radiator cap, had a two-cylinder engine that was very easy to maintain. Since most farmers were their own mechanics, this ease of operation and repair was an important feature. The last two-cylinder engine was installed in 1960, ending forty years of distinction.**

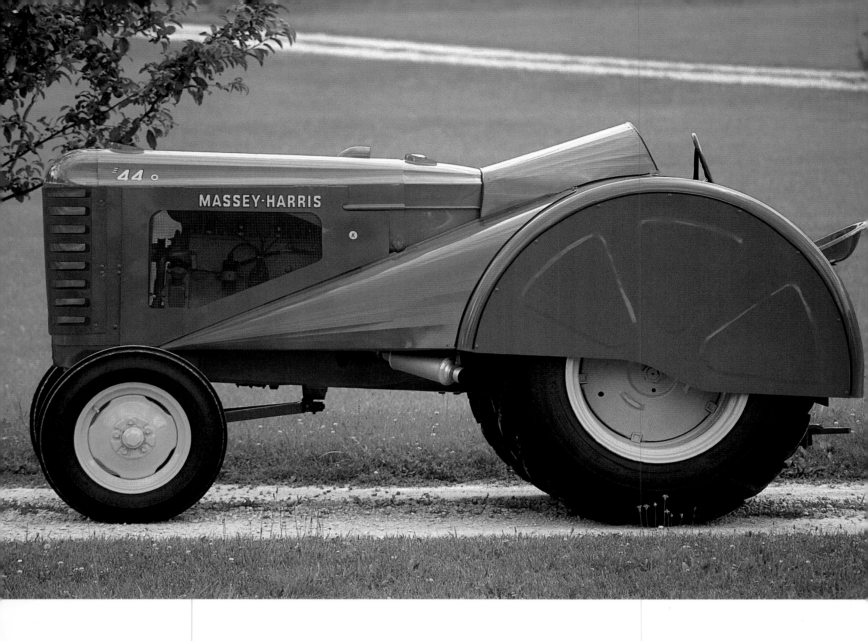

ABOVE: **Extremely attractive to enthusiasts and collectors, beautifully maintained tractors such as this Massey-Harris Model 44 orchard tractor command premium prices. This fine example is owned by Betty Lamb.**

RIGHT: **Massey-Harris is a venerable Canadian company, chartered in 1891. It entered the American marketplace in 1910 and has produced an outstanding line of tractors and agricultural equipment over the years. The Model 55 was introduced in 1948 and is noted as a tough and heavy machine.**

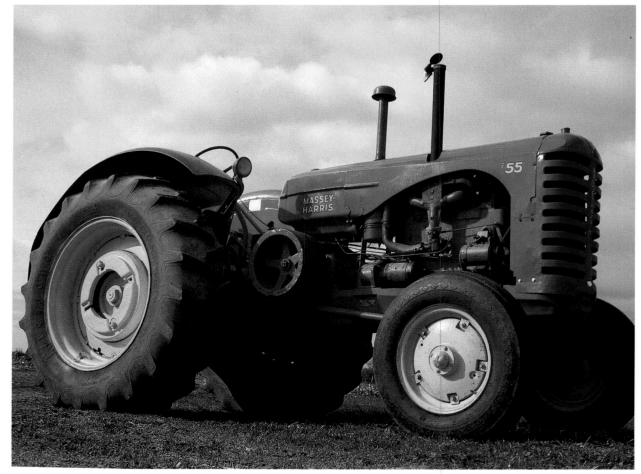

## The Golden Age Ends, a New Age Begins

The Golden Age of tractors came to a close around 1960. The Oliver Tractor Company, maker of tractordom's most beautiful machine, was sold, and the John Deere two-cylinder tractor, the famous Johnny Popper, disappeared from the marketplace. Both the Oliver 70 and the Johnny Popper are now greatly beloved by collectors. Minneapolis-Moline lost its corporate identity in 1969, as part of a merger with the White Motor Company of Cleveland, the organization that had already acquired Oliver. Massey-Ferguson continued in business. Allis-Chalmers nearly dropped out of sight but continued to build tractors until 1985. Since the major strength of Allis-Chalmers

*BELOW: Minneapolis-Moline tractors are easily recognized by their yellow-orange paint. Minnie-Mo began building tractors in the 1920s and introduced a few particularly innovative machines. This little example is a Model BF, first offered in 1951 and a terrific companion to the Deere L and the Farmall Cub.*

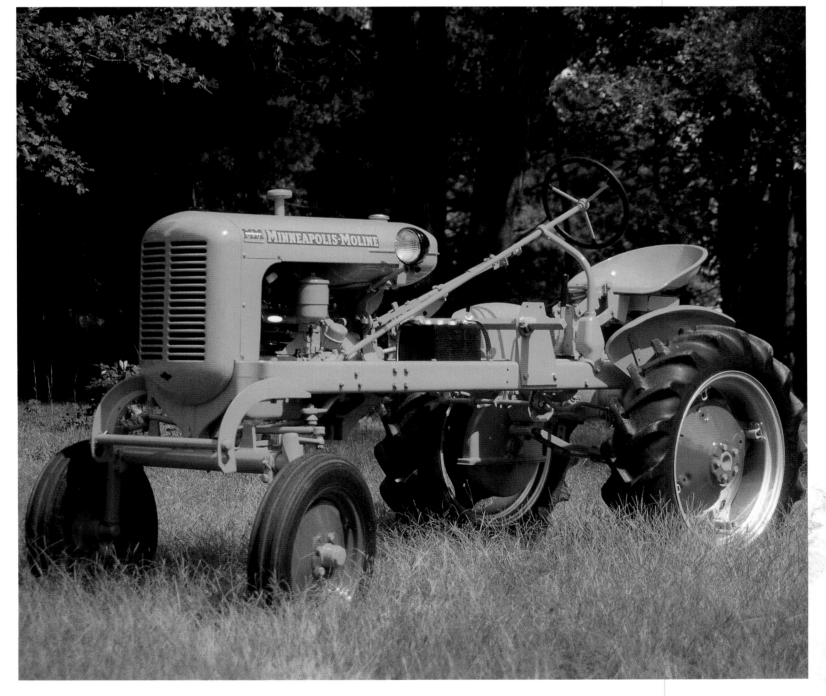

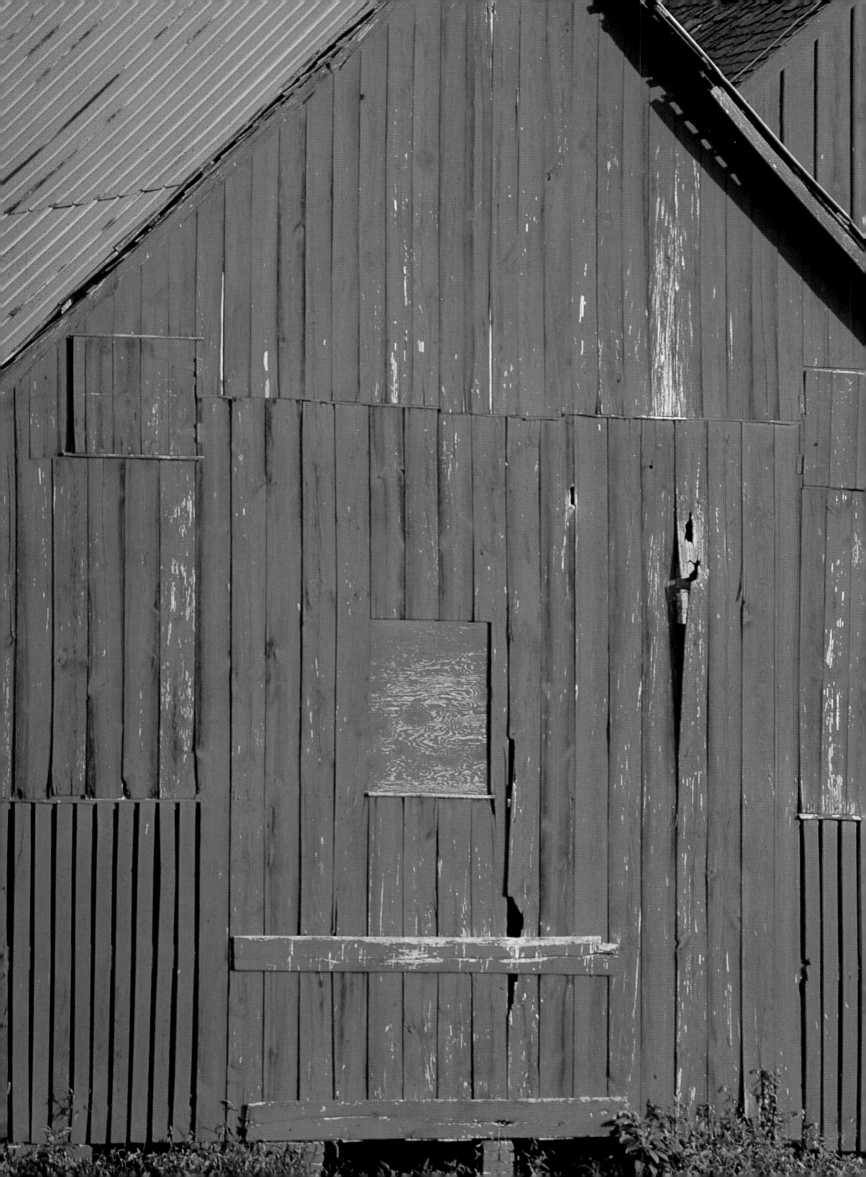

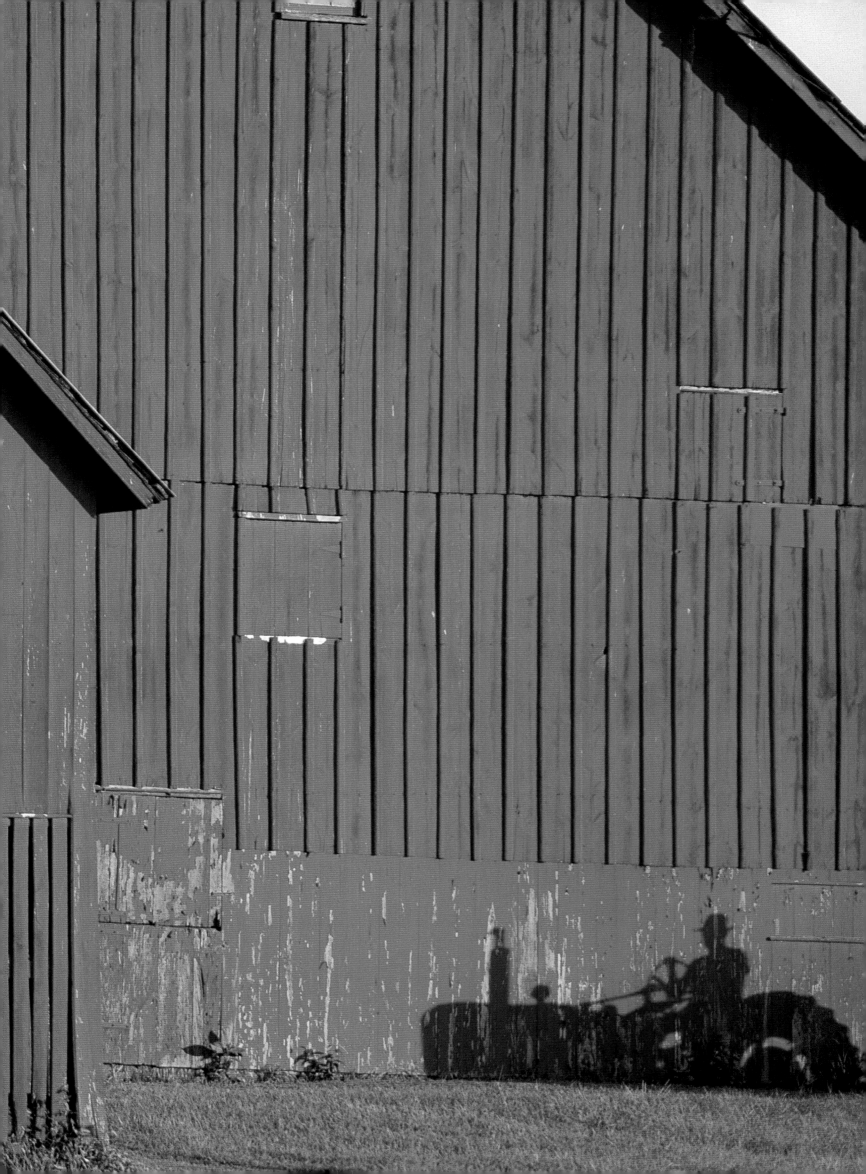

*PREVIOUS PAGES:*
**Tractors still cast long shadows on American farms. In many ways it is a simple machine, but it has allowed the American farmer to prosper and maintain independence.**

*RIGHT TOP:* **Collectors with space constraints like small tractors such as this Baby G, built by Allis-Chalmers between 1948 and 1955. Impeccably restored, this little guy is in the collection of Carmin Adams.**

*RIGHT BOTTOM:* **The Allis B first appeared around 1937 and was the smallest model offered until the appearance of the little Model G. Headquartered in Wisconsin, the Allis-Chalmers company produced a broad line of agricultural equipment.**

*OPPOSITE:* **While other tractors usually sport a metal seat with a distinctive pattern, many of the Allis tractors feature a seat with back support. This Model B belongs to collector Carmin Adams.**

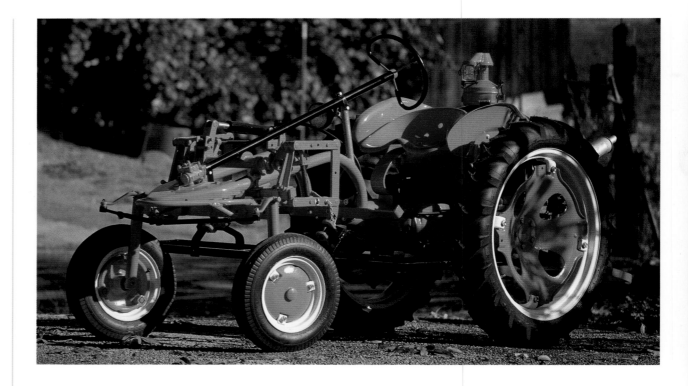

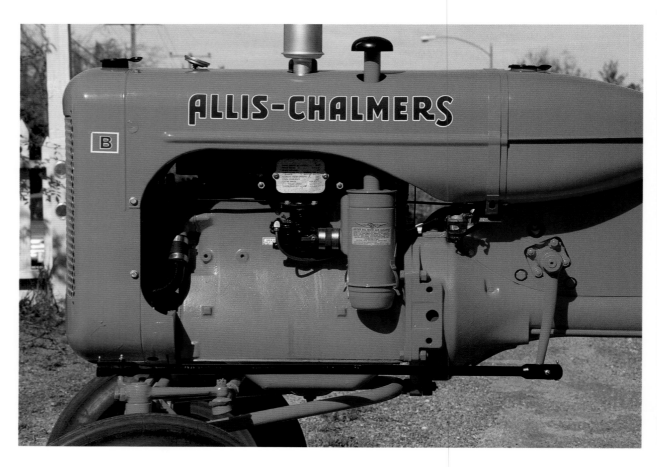

was not in tractors but in its other equipment, such as gleaners, it remained a continuing presence in the marketplace.

Tractors from other countries began showing up at American farm shows in the 1970s and 1980s, tractors made by manufacturers like Kubota from Japan, Leyland from England, and even an Italian, Lamborghini. Today, only two major American tractor builders are still standing: Case IH and John Deere.

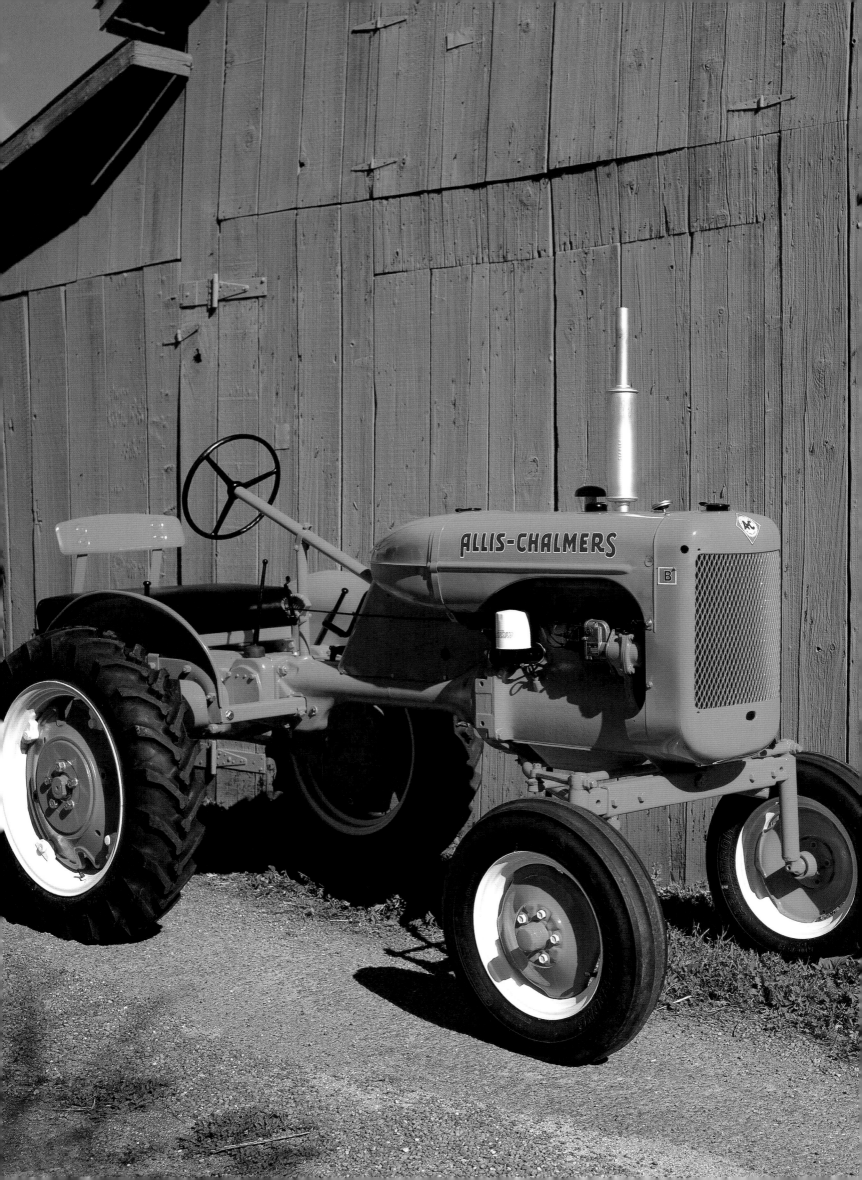

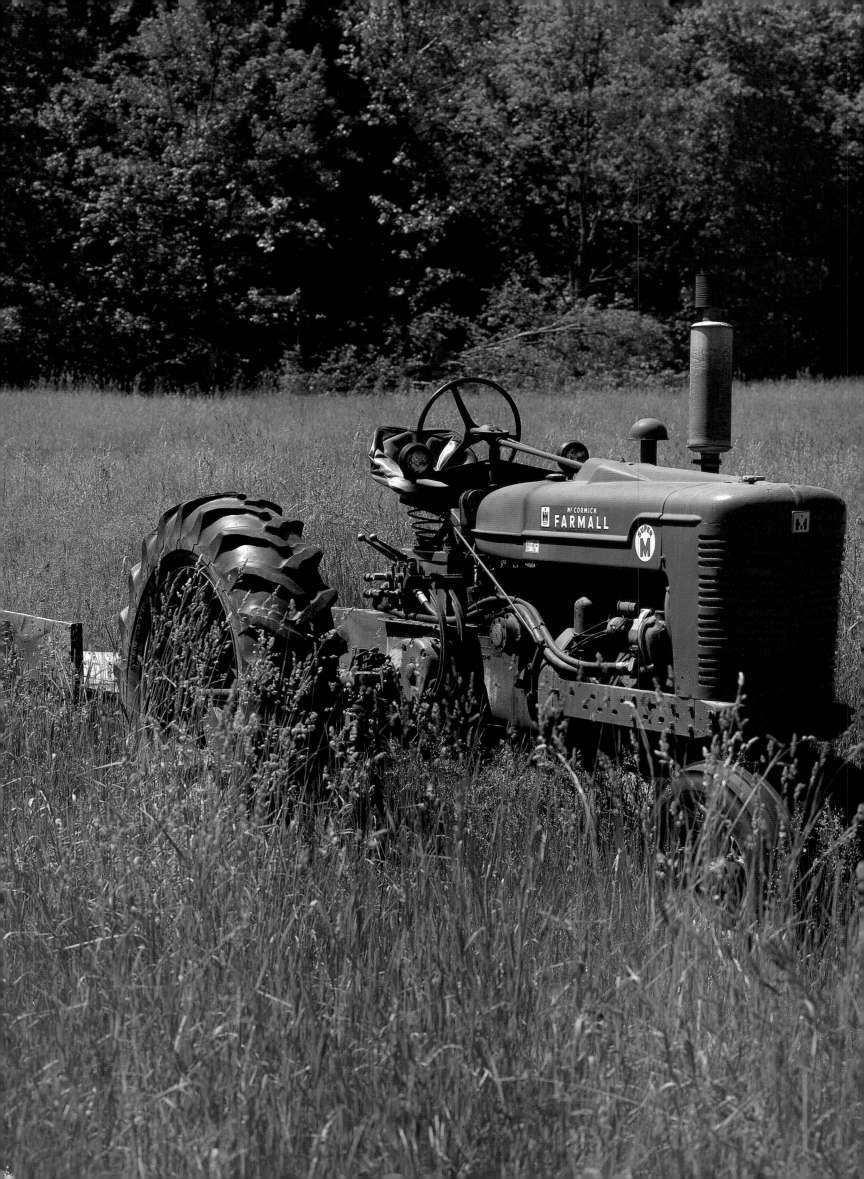

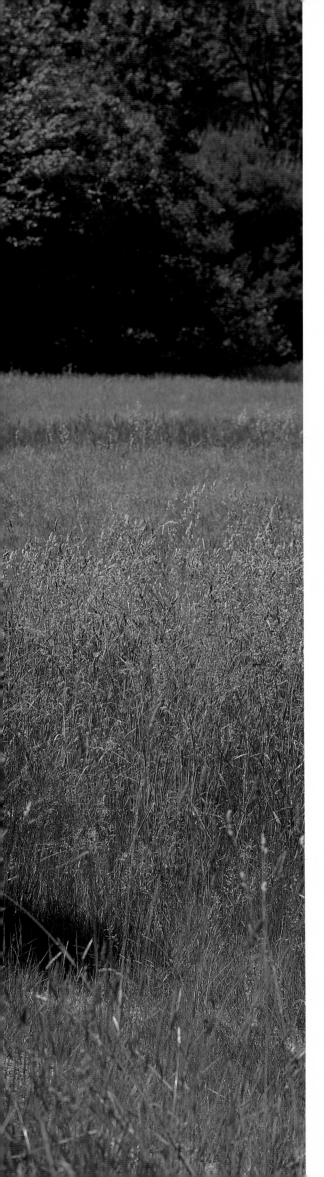

# NEW LIFE FOR OLD TRACTORS

*Chapter Five*

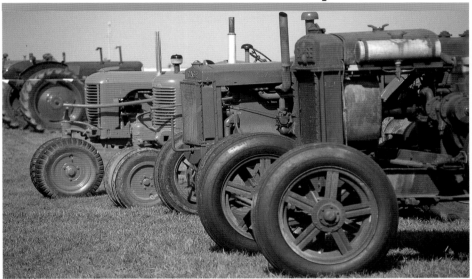

Two guys in coveralls were overheard at Tulare County's big annual antique tractor show.

"How many you bring this year?" asked the first.

"Well," considered his friend, "I think I brought nine. Had to make a couple of trips with the flatbed, but we got them all here."

"Which one are you going to ride in the parade today?"

"Whichever one I can get running. . . . "

There is a lot of interest, a lot of money, and a lot of emotion in collectible tractors these days. It's a curious situation—accumulations of large old machines that will never do another day's work now taking up a lot of space in the barn. Collecting tractors takes up a lot of time, too.

---

*LEFT:* **One of the great joys of owning a tractor like this McCormick Farmall Model M is the thrill of operating it.**

*ABOVE:* **Visit any fairgrounds during the summer and you are likely to find a tractor show with dozens of vintage machines in various stages of restoration.**

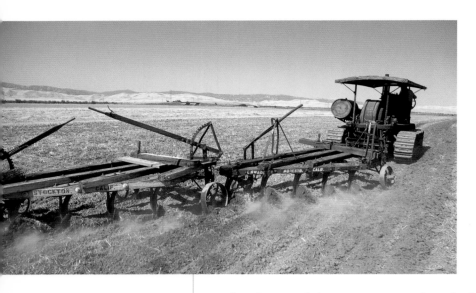

*ABOVE: This dusty vintage crawler is one of the most historically important machines in California. It is a 1925 Holt 75, demonstrating that it can still handle eight bottoms in the hot San Joaquin Valley. Irv Baker is the proud owner of this extraordinary machine.*

As with any collectible, rarity and condition determine the desirability and the price. In general, the same rules apply to a piece of Limoges china as to a vintage John Deere: the highest prices are paid for the older models in original condition.

But collecting and restoring tractors is a little more casual than attending art auctions. A fine piece of china with a chip or a crack may be nearly worthless, no matter how old or rare. By contrast, tractors are expected to have a few dings and dents, a new set of spark plugs, an upgraded set of tires, maybe even an engine rebuild. Getting forty years of work out of a tractor requires a little maintenance, so finding a tractor with its original, factory-fresh paint and little mileage is very suspicious. It may indicate that the previous owner bought a dud and was too embarrassed to admit it, or it may reveal a tractor that is too new to be true.

Prices for the old and the rare may seem astronomical. No one knows where the first Hart-Parr tractors are today. The Smithsonian is reluctant to put a price tag on Old Reliable, the oldest known gasoline tractor in existence. A beautiful, nicely restored orchard tractor from the 1940s can easily cost thirty thousand dollars, and similar machines command similar prices.

While every collector has favorites, some machines always generate a great deal of excitement because they are so rare. Many tractors, like the Happy Farmer, were albatrosses, poorly designed and quickly passed over years ago because better, cheaper machines were on the market. But today they all seem to attract a crowd when they are shown, usually because they represent a short-lived type of technology. Others, like the Fageol, could not survive the flood of Fordsons that saturated their market. Just a handful of Fageol tractors are now known to exist, and only one early Track-Pull.

Then there are the machines that have a wonderful story behind them. Some of these machines are very special because they form part of the local history of a community. The big Caterpillars could work in desert conditions where even mules would perish. Smaller Cats and Cletracs helped fight forest fires and assisted in the defense efforts of World War II. And many fruit farmers used only small crawlers, like the Cletrac or the Lindeman, because the treads would not damage delicate root systems. These machines contributed to their communities and are rightfully preserved in local museums across the nation.

Some machines capture collectors' imaginations because they were built as prototypes or experimental tractors. For years, collectors have been trying to locate the interesting early Oliver machines, built by the Altgelt brothers and now known only in photographs. Still shrouded in mystery is the legendary Black Tractor that Harry Ferguson built as a prototype for his experimental new draft control.

Then there is the "other" Ford, also a highly desirable vintage tractor. At one time there was actually a Ford Tractor Company that had nothing to do with Henry Ford. In 1916, a somewhat unscrupulous fellow named W. Baer Ewing wanted to sell tractors by capitalizing on the famous Ford name. So he found a man named Paul Ford and set up a tractor company in Minneapolis using the Ford name. Few machines were made by the copycat Ford Tractor Company, and the ones that did make it to the field were so badly built that they were generally unsatisfactory. Experiences like this led to the establishment of the Nebraska Tractor Tests, devised to test tractors before consumers could buy them. An unsuspecting Nebraska farmer named Wilmot Crozier had purchased a tractor that did not meet his expectations. Disenchanted, he persuaded his state congressman to establish a test lab at the University of Nebraska in order to protect Nebraska farmers.

The Nebraska lab became the most important testing lab in America, providing the tractor buyer and the manufacturer with reliable and impartial data. The lab eventually helped put unscrupulous and inept tractor builders out of business. But some of these bad early tractors are still around, now considered collectible curiosities. The bogus "Fords" still show up at exhibits and they always collect a crowd. There seems to be a market for everything.

## John Deere Collectibles

By far, the largest group of collectors today belong to the John Deere fan clubs. There is a lot to collect, since Deeres are such popular machines all across the country.

Despite the tremendous numbers of John Deere tractors in the field, many of the more exotic models are quite rare. John Deere offered a very wide range of models and options, so some of its tractors were actually built in very limited numbers. The Model 530 LP, for instance, was equipped to run on LP gas. The books show that only about four hundred of this model were built, so even though it is a relatively new machine, built after 1960, collectors are still interested in acquiring it.

*BELOW: Looking like an ordinary Deere GP, this extremely rare Model B is prized for its wide wheel placement and its high crop stance. Collector John Boehm bought it for his wife as an engagement present.*

## Collecting Orchard Tractors

One favorite group of tractors among collectors is the orchard tractor, a rare and fascinating type of machine designed for use in orchards and vineyards. Always made in limited numbers, orchard tractors are difficult to find and are eagerly sought for their styling and because of their scarcity.

Nearly every major tractor manufacturer had an orchard tractor in its product line at one time or another. The orchard tractor differs significantly from a row-crop machine, requiring the builder to make quite a few changes to serve this market segment. Orchard tractors are lower to the ground than most machines and the seat sits well below the hood, a design that protects the driver from overhanging branches when working close to the trees.

The wheel covers and engine covers of the orchard tractor are completely enclosed, to prevent branches from snagging on the tractor as it passes underneath. Mufflers and exhaust stacks are short, too, to keep them from being snapped off by the trees. This type of tractor frequently has special wheels or tires to provide traction in sandy soil and also to prevent damage to trees with shallow root structures. All these features contribute to the desirability of a vintage orchard tractor.

Besides the fact that limited numbers of orchard tractors were manufactured, several other factors make them rare. Since many fruit farmers removed the protective cowling and the flared wheel covers, it is difficult to find a representative orchard tractor with all its original sheet metal. In addition, many farmers used the tops of the fenders to carry bags of lime, keeping the lime handy to apply to the crop when needed. The lime eventually ate through the paint and the sheet metal on the tops of the fender, though, so it's unusual to find a good orchard tractor without a bald spot on the top of its fenders. And, beyond that, fruit farms and vineyards are generally found in warmer climates, where tractors are often left outdoors.

All that sunshine is hard on the complexion, even for a tractor.

Several kinds of orchard tractors are particularly rare and only a few are known to survive. One is the Bean Track-Pull, a small machine built for orchard and vineyard use in the Santa Clara Valley. Its tricycle design features a treadlike front wheel and two widespread rear wheels for stability. Manufactured for only two years, the little tractor was built just before World War I. The Bean Company, an agricultural equipment company in San Jose, California, then became part of what is now known as FMC, one of the world's largest producers of tanks and

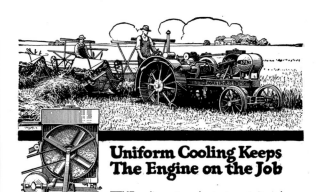

### Uniform Cooling Keeps The Engine on the Job

THE cooling system of a tractor gets its real test during the heat of harvest and early fall plowing.

it is then that you can rely upon the Waterloo Boy—the pump, fan and radiator system of cooling always keeps the engine on the job.

A centrifugal pump, four-blade fan, and large size, honey-comb type radiator insure positive cooling on the Waterloo Boy.

### WATERLOO BOY
#### BURNS KEROSENE COMPLETELY

To secure uniform power you must have uniform cooling. The pump, fan and radiator system used on the Waterloo Boy positively assures uniformity in circulating cooling water.

It holds the engine at the right temperature for proper lubrication, and maintains sufficient heat to insure complete combustion and full power from the fuel.

An even temperature is maintained at all operating speeds because the speed of the pump and fan is automatically controlled by the speed of the engine.

You get a big radiator on the Waterloo Boy. It holds thirteen gallons. You won't find it necessary to stop in the field every few hours on a hot day and fill it.

The cooling system is but one of the Waterloo Boy's superior features. Its simplicity and accessibility, its powerful 12-25 H. P. engine, its ability to burn kerosene and burn it right, its Hyatt roller bearings that eliminate friction, and a drawbar shift lever that gives you the correct line of draft on all tools, all contribute to make it a real farm tractor.

We want you to read a booklet describing the Waterloo Boy. Write for it today. Address John Deere, Moline, Illinois, and ask for booklet WB-648.

John Deere Implements, Waterloo Boy Tractors and Kerosene Engines are distributed from all important Trading Centers. Sold by John Deere Dealers everywhere.

### JOHN DEERE
#### THE TRADE MARK OF QUALITY MADE FAMOUS BY GOOD IMPLEMENTS

*ABOVE: A John Deere advertisement for its Waterloo Boy tractor, a machine designed to run on kerosene.*

*BELOW: A Massey-Harris orchard tractor is a rare and unusual machine. Headquartered in Toronto, Ontario, the company was noted for providing durable machines for the Canadian market.*

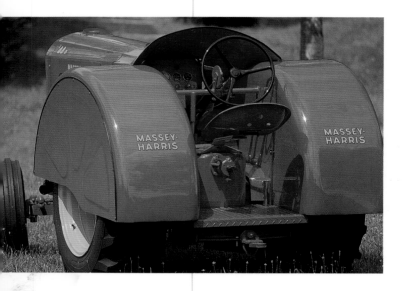

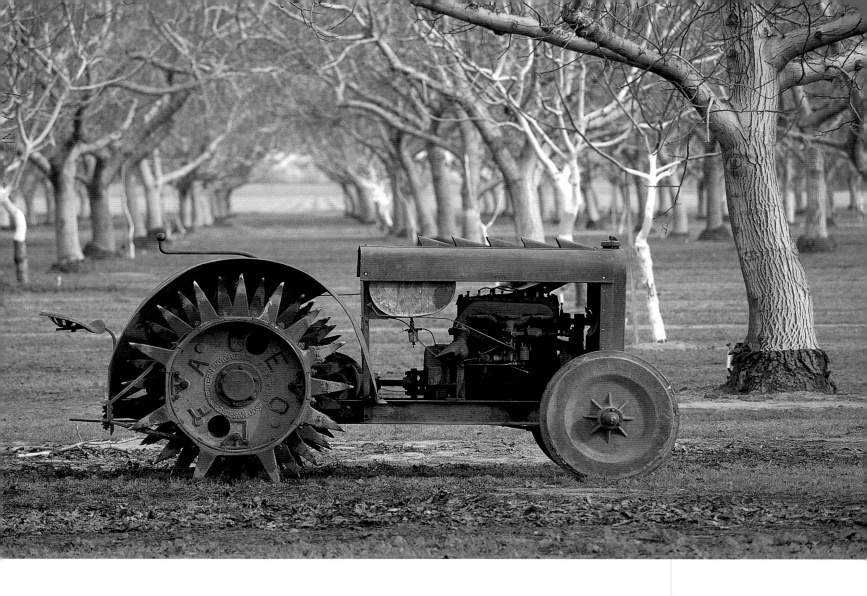

tracked military vehicles. The Bean Track-Pull represents a period in American history when plowshares were beaten into swords.

Another rare and interesting orchard tractor with a distinctive history is the Fageol, a machine produced for only four years. Like the Hart-Parr, the Waterloo Boy, and many important early machines, this tractor has its roots in Iowa. Although the machine itself was built in California, its two designers—the Fageol brothers, Frank and William—got their start building vehicles at their home near Des Moines, Iowa, before the turn of the twentieth century.

The brothers were extremely interested in automobile manufacturing and founded a business in San Francisco just before the big earthquake of 1906. After the quake, they relocated to downtown Oakland, California, where they opened a shop. They manufactured one of the most reliable engines of the day, which they christened the Victory engine, a large, tough powerhouse, suitable for use in airplanes and boats. The military bought it for aviation purposes in World War I.

The Fageols built some of the earliest "touring cars" or buses, large limousine-type vehicles ideal for sightseeing. One of the first West Coast builders of large vehicles, the brothers also built delivery trucks and vans for hauling heavy loads. Known throughout California as one of the most successful and productive vehicle builders, they were approached by local farmers to build a tractor, too, one that would be especially suitable for the orchards and vineyards in their local area.

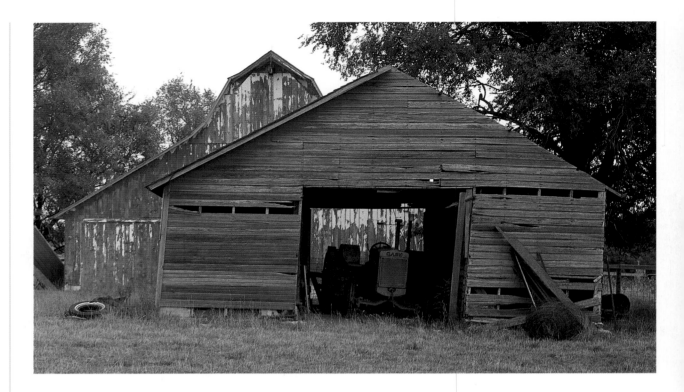

RIGHT: *Sometimes you can spot a rare vintage tractor from the road, like this Case seen in the shelter of a northern Missouri barn. The owner of this machine enjoys considering the offers of hopeful enthusiasts who think they have made an important discovery.*

The brothers were talked into working with the design developed by an acquaintance named Louis Bill. Bill was from the vineyard and orchard region of nearby Napa, California, and had already been issued a patent for his tractor design. A small company was formed to build the tractor, with Bill serving as president.

The Fageol was built low to avoid snagging on delicate orchard branches and featured spiked wheels for greater traction in sandy soil. But it was too heavy and too expensive when compared with its local competition, which, surprisingly, turned out to be the widely distributed Fordson. Less than ten Fageol tractors are known to have survived.

The Yuba Ball Tread from Marysville, California, and the Johnson Tractor from Sunnyvale are just two more early and very rare orchard tractors, the kinds of machines that collectors covet and hoard. Prized for their early and innovative technology of using treads rather than wheels, these machines were truly the product of the individual inventors' genius. Later machines would be shaped by their competitors' sales and marketing departments, rather than by engineers with a vision all their own.

## Getting Started in Collecting

OPPOSITE: *Most of the early farm machinery was so well made that, with proper care, it could potentially last for decades. The J.I. Case Company was the first builder with a materials-testing laboratory to ensure the quality of their parts. A well-designed and well-built machine is a joy to own.*

Tractor collecting is one of those hobbies that can sneak up on the unsuspecting. Hang around tractor shows, and you will hear a lot of "lost dog" stories about tractors. They go something like this: "There we were, driving along the back road, when we saw a sign that said, 'Estate Sale.' We didn't bid on anything, but on the way out I noticed an old, rusty frame at the side of the yard. The owner saw me

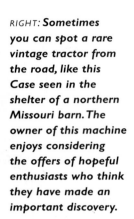

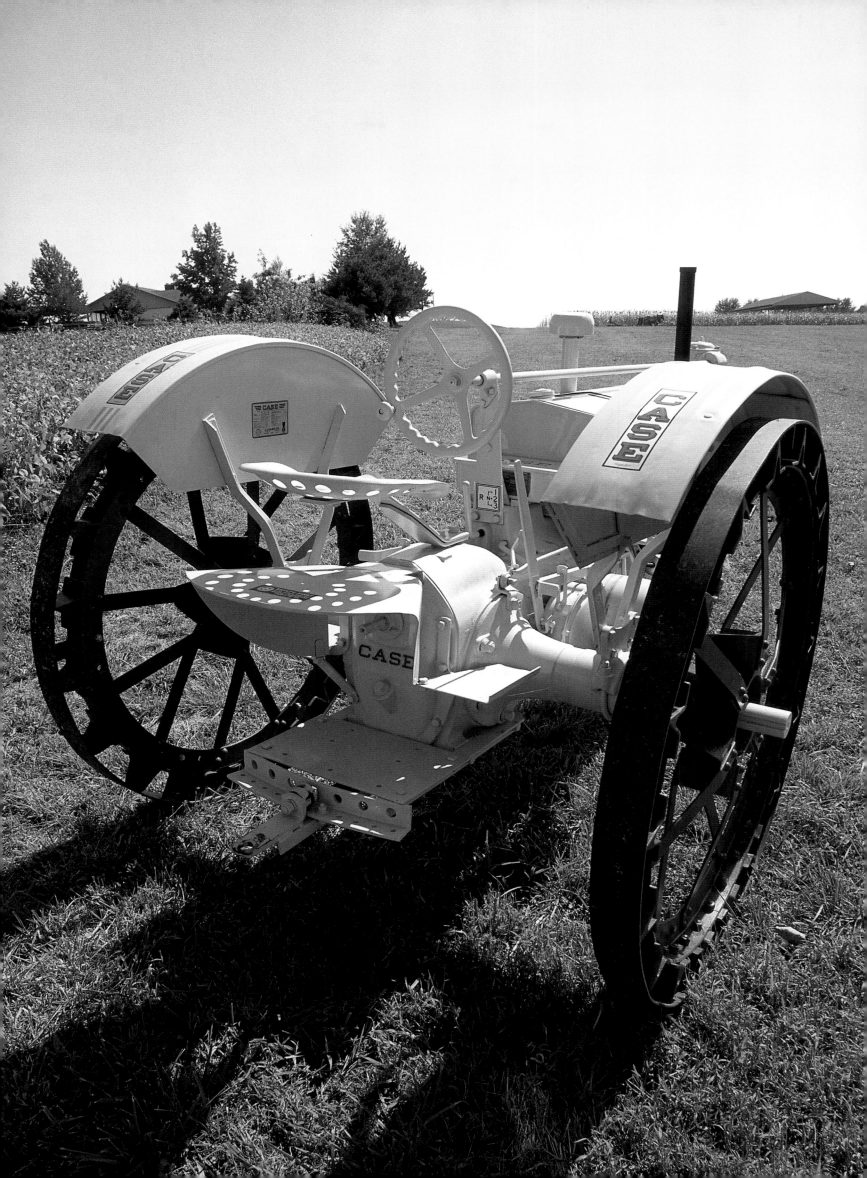

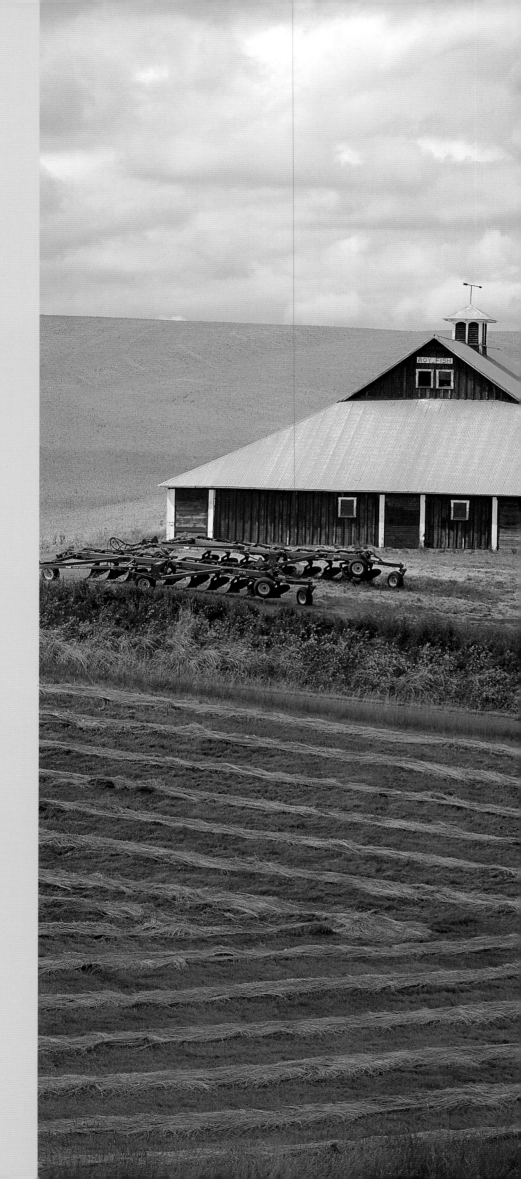

FROM *THE KANSAS CITY STAR,* AUGUST 21, 2000:

# DOWN ON THE FARM IS WHERE MANY OF US WEREN'T MEANT TO BE

BY BILL TAMMEUS

BOTH MY PARENTS grew up on farms. I didn't. Well, there's debate in my family about whether I grew up at all, but let's not go there.

When I was a boy my grandparents still operated the farms on which my parents spent their childhoods. The two branches of my family, thus, were either marvels of consistency or they lacked imagination. I never quite figured out which.

Anyway, this all meant that I was able to hang around this or that piece of farm machinery when I was a youngster.

I loved farm machinery. It made me imagine that it was possible to coax copious amounts of crops out of the land without the kind of drudgery that had made slavery economically justifiable to so many people.

Even today, I love farm machinery. My uncle farms the land my grandfather farmed, and I enjoy stopping by there now and then to see monstrous metal equipment ready to lurch into corn and soybean fields.

Which is why it rather pleased me to learn that the American Society of Mechanical Engineers recently cited agricultural mechanization as one of the greatest mechanical engineering achievements of the twentieth century.

In case you're keeping tabs, others in the group's top ten list of mechanical engineering feats of the century were: integrated circuit mass production, computer-aided design and manufacturing technology, bioengineering, codes and standards, air conditioning and refrigeration, the

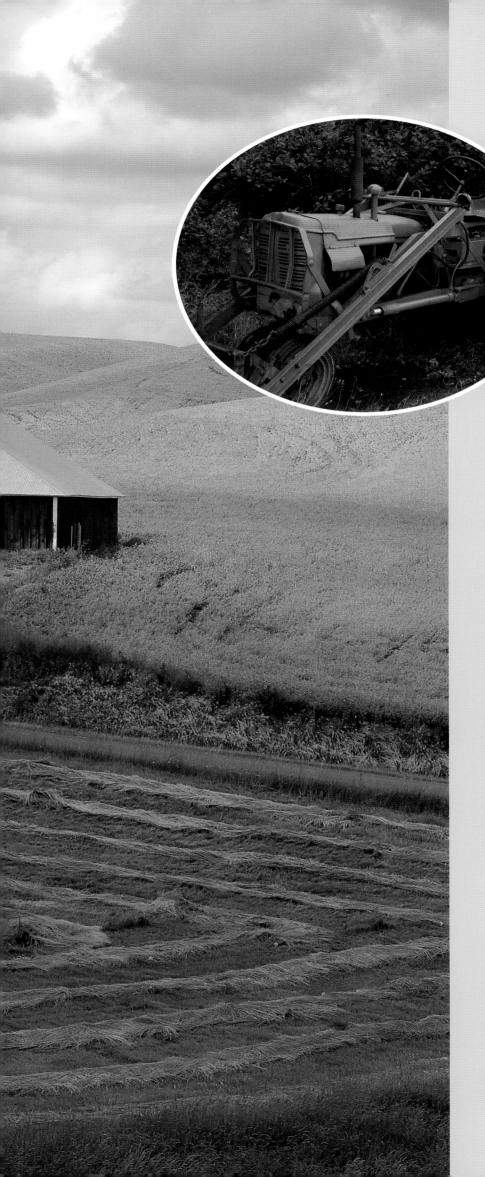

airplane, power generation, the Apollo space program, the automobile and limitless chicken parts.

Oh, that's one too many. Scratch chicken parts. That's on my list, not the engineers'. The list of cool farm machinery almost has to start with the tractor. And, to me, the neatest thing about tractors is that they can be driven off to county fairs and entered in tractor-pulling contests.

When I was a kid, I watched maybe 142,566 tractor-pulling contests at our local county fair and would cheer the loudest for the ones that did the highest wheelies.

I know now that my attraction to these contests was a mark of my immaturity and my fascination with the amusing and frivolous use of serious equipment.

But, it turns out, I was learning how vital all that noisy power was to my own future as a non-farmer.

Back at the start of the twentieth century, says *Mechanical Engineering* magazine, one American farmer fed about 2.5 people. (No, I don't know what half a people is, so don't ask.) But one hundred years later, that one farmer (well, not that very one, who'd be 130-plus years old or more) feeds ninety-seven Americans plus thirty-two other people living abroad.

As I say, that means I don't have to be a farmer. Or as *Mechanical Engineering* magazine says, this mechanical revolution released "the population to pursue intellectual, cultural and social development that has resulted in our modern society."

Well, I think that claim is a little broad. I mean, I don't think we need to blame farm machinery for all our bad TV, violent movies, suburban shopping malls, talk show hosts and whatnot.

But it is true that because I don't have to grow my own food by hand—or with a hand from mules or horses—I am free to write columns pointing out that I am free to write columns because I don't have to grow my own food by hand.

And you're free to sit around reading such columns instead of trudging out to your spaghetti (or whatever) field and pulling weeds. If not for that kind of progress, do you realize you and I might own hand-pulled manure spreaders?

*LEFT: **Once cultivated by hundreds of horses and dozens of men, our farmland can now be harvested by one man and a tractor.***

*INSET: **Every improvement in farm machinery, such as the addition of this loader on the front of a tractor, has resulted in tremendous efficiency in agricultural production.***

RIGHT: **Case and International Harvester have now combined forces and are known as Case IH. With an enclosed cab, air conditioning, roll bars, and cup holders, this modern tractor is a joint effort and a fine engineering accomplishment.**

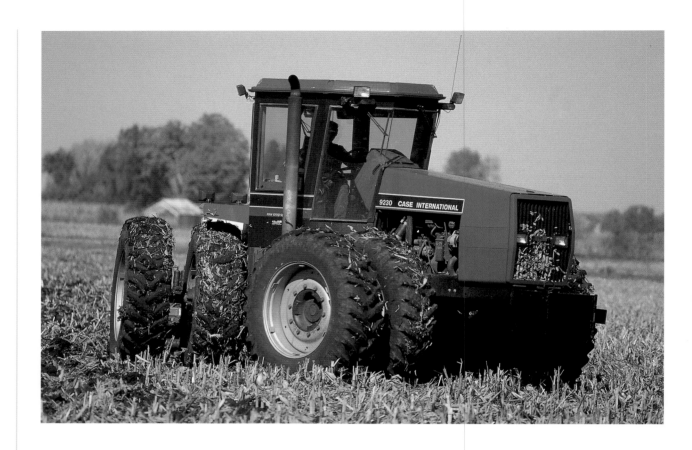

BELOW: **Many young farmers, boys and girls, first learned to drive on a tractor like this. Such an experience seems unlikely on a modern tractor like the one pictured above.**

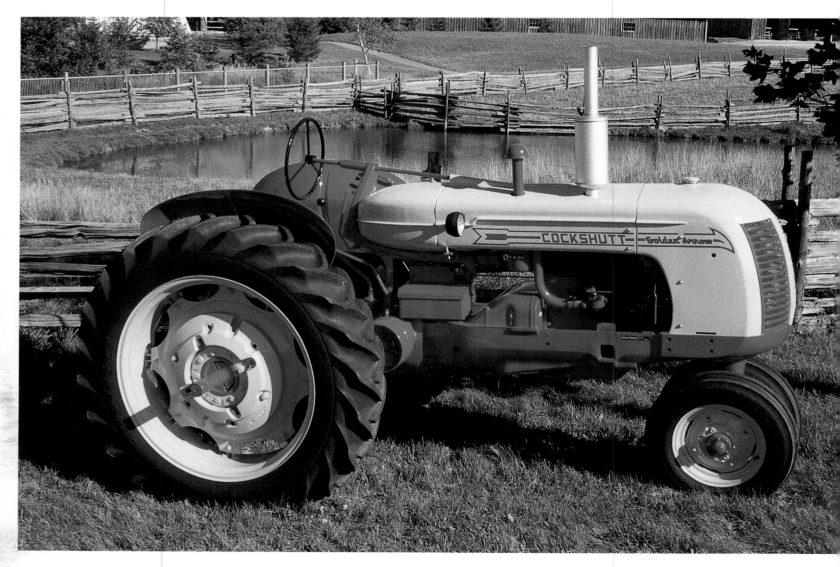

looking at it and said I ought to take a peek in the shed." You can fill in the rest of the story. Another poor innocent, bitten by the tractor bug. Like the stray dog, tractors somehow follow you home.

The tractor want ads are also hard to pass up. Want to take a chance on a 1946 John Deere Model B for only nine hundred, as is? The ad says that it runs. Hmmm. Maybe it only runs downhill. At least that might mean that it isn't frozen up. It pays to be an eternal optimist in the tractor game.

Well, most tractor collectors do, indeed, seem to be optimists. Their first goal is always to get it running again. Such devotion, such single-mindedness, such dedication . . . in some cases it takes them years to assemble all the appropriate parts. Weekends in junkyards, months in the shop, but finally the moment of truth arrives. A little gasoline sloshed in the carburetor and, with any kind of luck, a running tractor! Making the machine presentable is sometimes another story.

## Other Paths to Follow

In addition to finding an old tractor and fixing it up, enthusiasts have several other outlets for their interests. Summertime is the season for tractor pulls, contests pitting one tractor against another in a test of strength and endurance. Old tractors that have been modified for pulling are always fun to watch.

Other collectors specialize in antique farm toys and toy tractors. The manufacture of miniature reproductions has become big business. Some toy companies even make little steam engines that actually work.

There is also a sizable industry these days in the manufacture of replacement parts for old tractors. Pick up any tractor magazine and you will find someone who can repair and rebore your pistons, rebuild a carburetor, and

*FOLLOWING PAGES:* **Another revolutionary concept in agricultural design from Oliver, the Oliver 70 with integrated implements. By attaching the implements through the frame rather than dragging them behind, the turning radius was shortened considerably.**

*BELOW:* **Tractor collecting is an international hobby. This one-cylinder Field Marshall, built in England, is proudly owned by California collector Robbie Soults.**

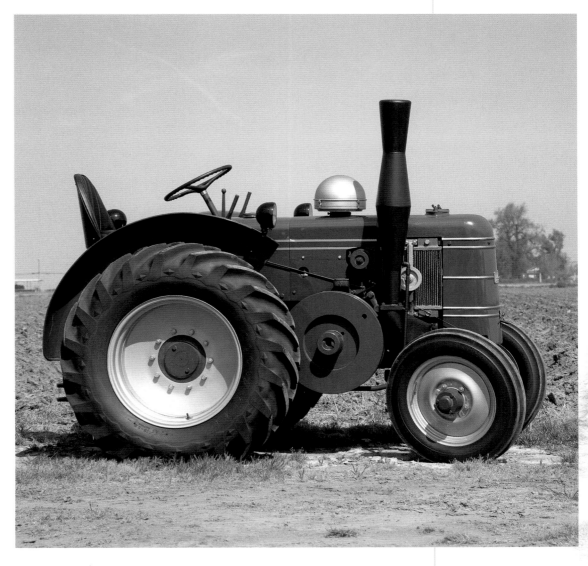

103

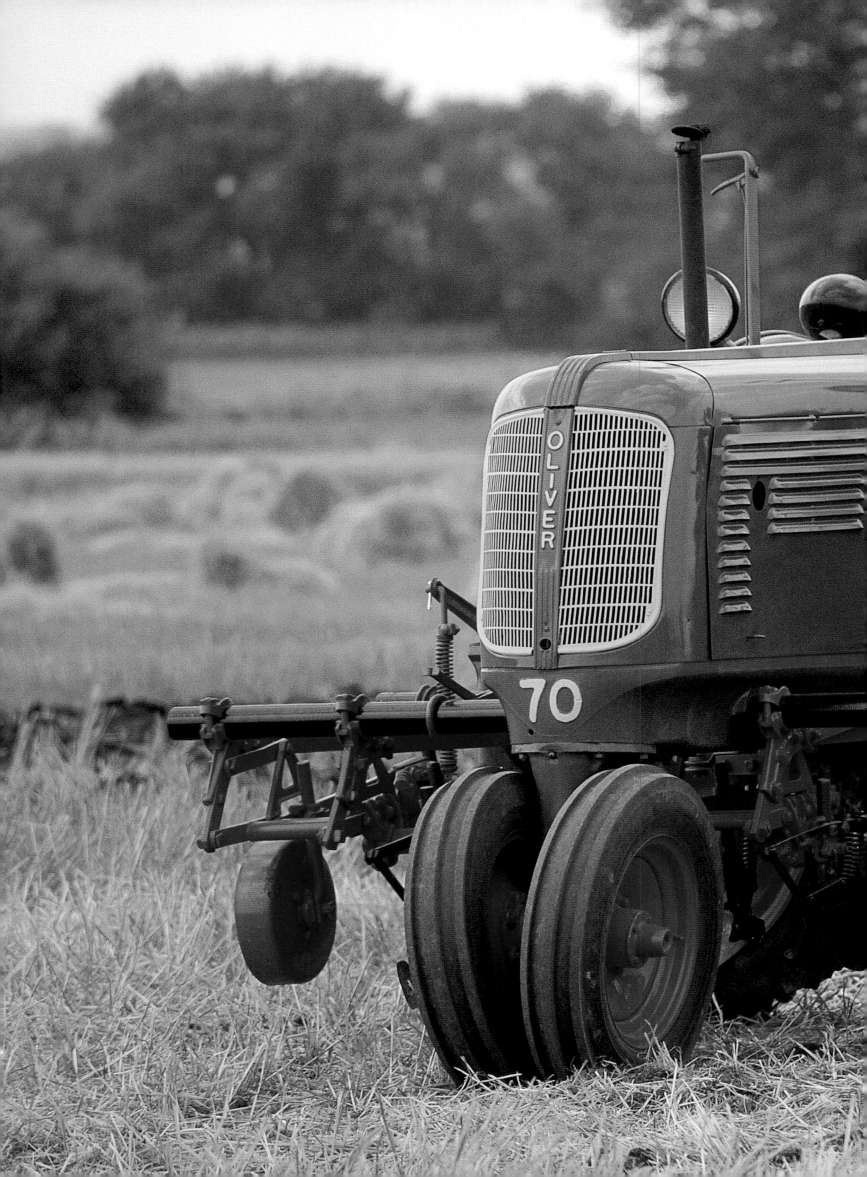

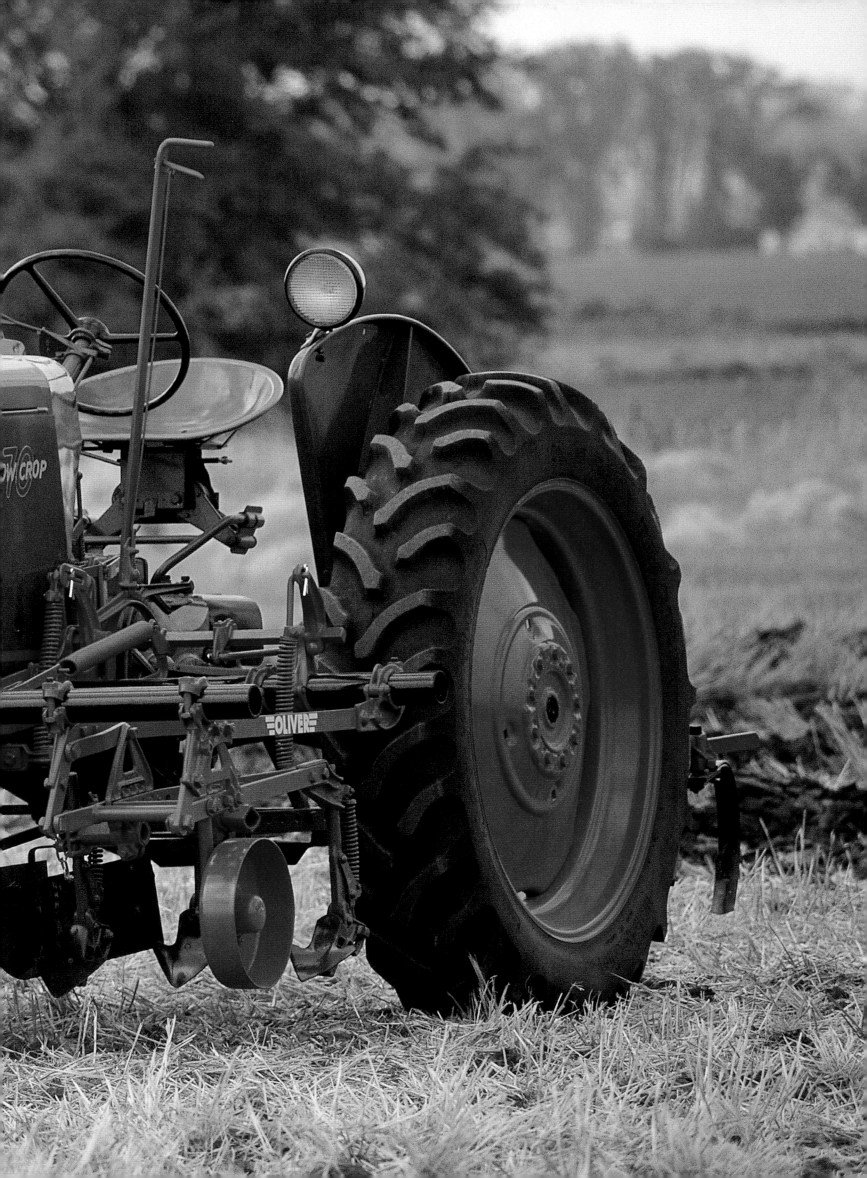

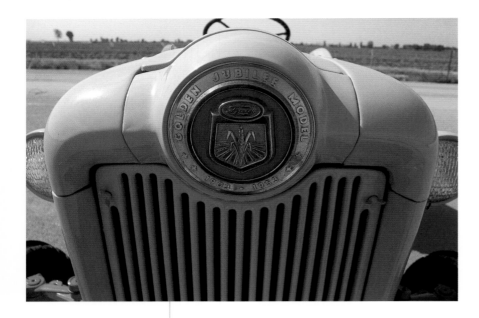

ABOVE: *The Jubilee Ford is something of a bittersweet machine for many collectors. Appearing well after Ford's death, it marked the end of an era when tractors were priced for the common man.*

RIGHT: *Tractor enthusiasts frequently show their treasures at county and state fairs and other events. More than just an exhibition, a show is an opportunity to swap information, buy and sell spare parts, and locate the next candidate for the collection.*

OPPOSITE: *Incredibly elegant styling is the hallmark of this Porsche-Diesel, one of a handful of foreign tractors shown at the big vintage tractor show held in Tulare County, California, every spring. Beautiful tractors like the Porsche encourage collectors to expand their horizons.*

restore a magneto. Need new upholstery, decals, or a steering wheel? They can usually be found, some of them in good-as-new condition.

Tractor collectors are special people, and their interest in their machines usually runs much deeper than a passion for mere possession. A tractor is a tool, made to be productive. Many collectors restore their tractors in order to use them. They enjoy finding vintage implements for their machines and then taking them to the field. Many farmers organize "play days" on which they drag all their machines to one location and take turns operating the old equipment. These activities and these collectors are what has kept our tractor heritage alive.

The year 2003 marks the one hundredth anniversary of the first appearance of the American farm tractor. No longer sent to the scrap heap, the vintage tractor is a reminder of the work and the values at the core of our national identity and our economic well-being. We should extend our heartfelt appreciation to those who make it possible.

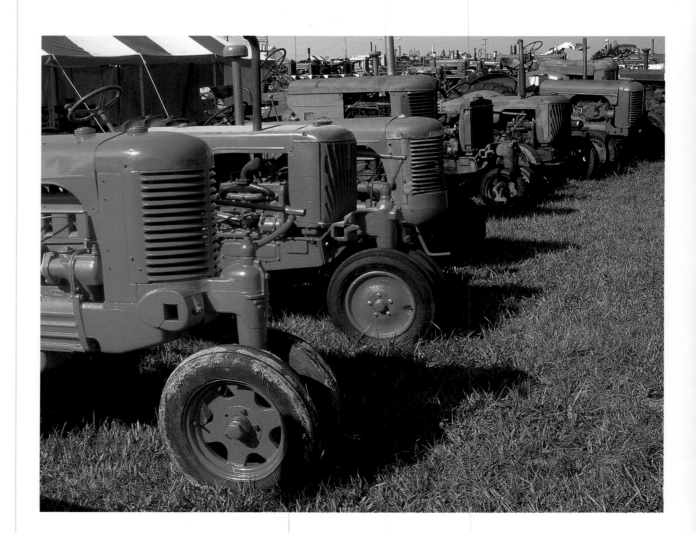

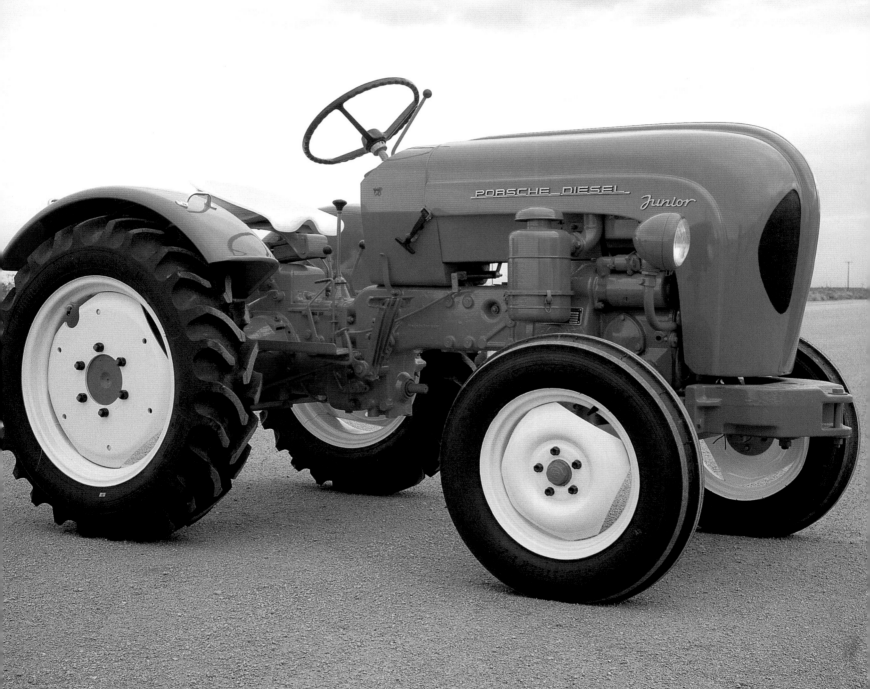

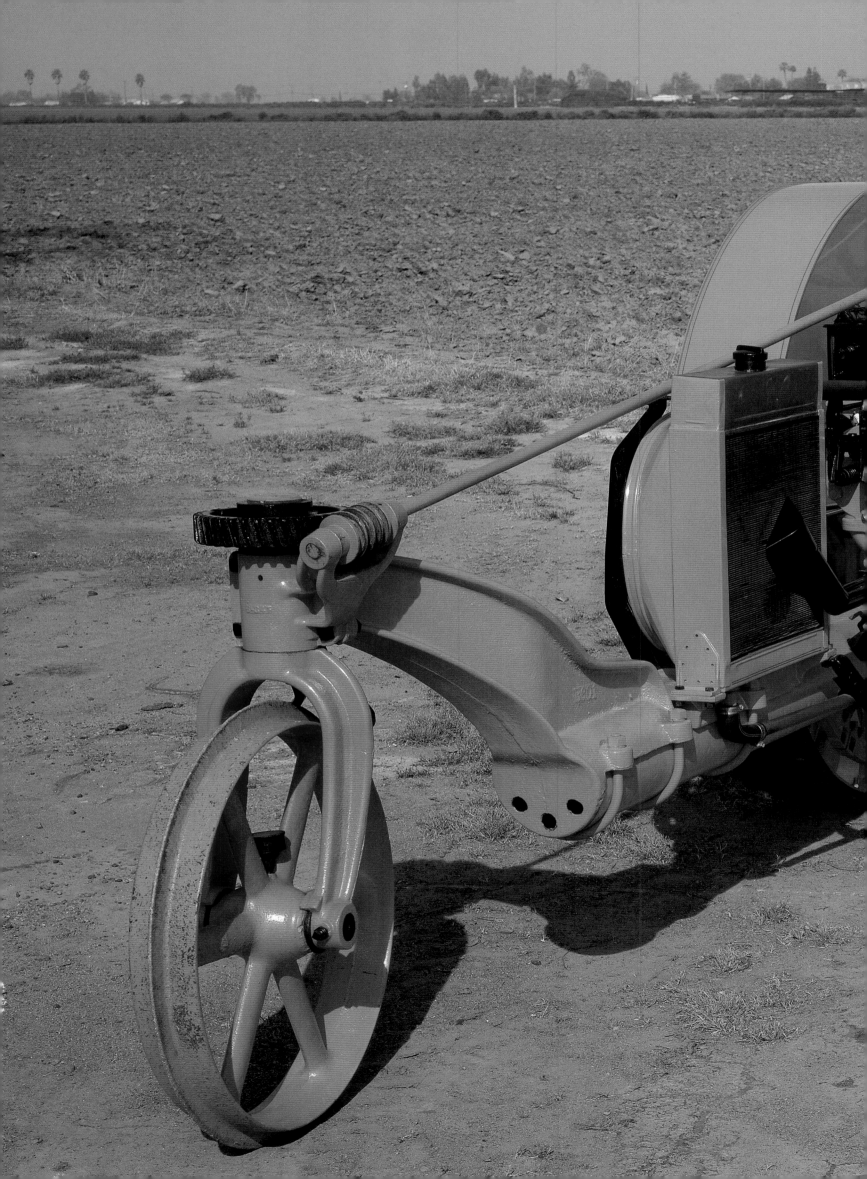

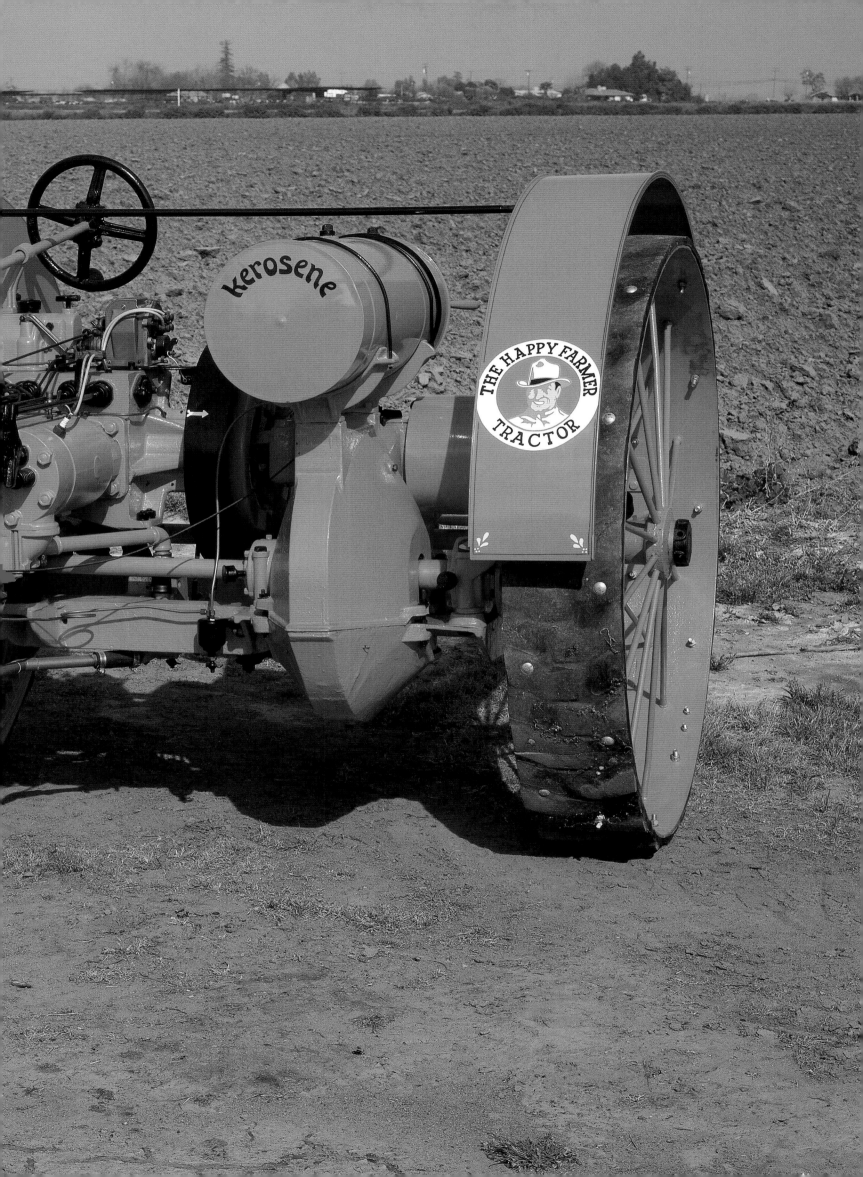

# Bibliography

Broehl, Wayne. *John Deere's Company.* New York: Doubleday & Company, 1984.

Buescher, Walter M. *The Plow Peddler.* Macomb, Ill.: Glenbridge Publishing Company, 1992.

Currie, Barton W. *The Tractor.* Philadelphia: Curtis Publishing Company, 1916.

Erb, Dave, and Eldon Brumbaugh. *Full Steam Ahead: J.I. Case Tractors and Equipment 1842–1955.* St. Joseph, Mich.: American Society of Agricultural Engineers, 1993.

Gray, R.B. *The Agricultural Tractor, 1855–1950.* St. Joseph, Mich.: American Society of Agricultural Engineers, 1975.

Halberstadt, April. *Case Photographic History.* Osceola, Wisc.: Motorbooks International, 1995.

———. *Farm Tractors.* New York: Metrobooks, 1998.

———. *Oliver Photographic History.* Osceola, Wisc.: Metrobooks International, 1997.

Halberstadt, Hans. *Steam Tractors.* Osceola, Wisc.: Motorbooks International, 1996.

Holmes, Michael S. *J.I. Case: The First 150 Years.* Racine, Wisc.: Case Corporation, 1992.

King, Alan C. *Massey-Harris: Data Book No. 6.* Delaware, Ohio: Massey Harris Company, 1992.

Leffingwell, Randy. *Caterpillar.* Osceola, Wisc.: Motorbooks International, 1994.

McMillan, Don. *John Deere Tractors and Equipment, Volume One, 1837–1959.* St. Joseph, Mich.: American Society of Agricultural Engineers, 1988.

Miller, Lynn. *Workhorse Handbook.* Reedsport, Ore.: Lynn R. Miller, 1981.

Wendel, C.H. *Encyclopedia of American Farm Tractors.* Osceola, Wisc.: Crestline Publishing, Company, 1979.

———. *Nebraska Tractor Tests Since 1920.* Osceola, Wisc.: Crestline Publishing Company, 1985.

———. *Unusual Vintage Tractors.* Iola, Wisc.: Krause Publications, 1996.

Wik, Reynold M. *Benjamin Holt and Caterpillar.* St. Joseph, Mich.: American Society of Agricultural Engineers, 1984.

# Antique Tractor Resources

*For more information about tractors, their history, and their collectors, consult the following sources:*

The Antique Tractor Information Society (ATIS) maintains an informative Web site on the Internet: *<www.atis.net>*

A number of magazines are devoted to the subject. The best general-interest one is:

*Antique Power Magazine*
Pat Ertel, Editor
P.O. Box 838
Yellow Springs, OH 45387

There are also periodicals devoted to each manufacturer:

*Green Magazine (John Deere)*
R. and C. Hain, Editors
Rural Route 1
Bee, NE 68314

*Hart-Parr/Oliver Collector*
P.O. Box 685
Charles City, IA 50616

*M-M Correspoder*
 (Minneapolis-Moline)
Roger Mohr, Editor
Route 1, Box 153
Vail, IA 51465

*9N-2N-8N Newsletter* (Ford)
G.W. Rinaldi, Editor
Route 2, Box 2427
Vinton, OH 45686

*Old Allis News* (Allis-Chalmers)
Nan Jones, Editor
10925 Love Road
Belleview, MI 49021

*Red Power* (International
 Harvester)
Daryl Miller, Editor
Box 277
Battle Creek, IA 51006

PREVIOUS PAGES: **The Happy Farmer was a surprising design, a tricycle tractor with offset steering. But this machine was too radical, as well as unreliable, and soon disappeared from the market.**

# Index

## Photo Credits

Corbis: pp. 8, 26

©Kevin Fleming: pp. 88–89

©David R. Frazier: 24–25

©Hans Halberstadt: pp. 2–3, 5, 6–7, 10, 12, 16–17, 17 right, 18, 19, 20 top, 20 bottom, 21, 22, 23, 27 top, 28–29, 31, 32–33, 34, 35, 36–37, 40–41, 42 top, 43, 44 top, 44 bottom, 45, 47 top, 47 bottom, 48, 49 top, 50, 51 top, 52 top, 52 bottom, 53, 54–55, 55 right, 56, 57, 58, 59, 60 left, 60–61, 63 top, 63 bottom, 64, 65 top, 66–67, 67 inset, 68, 69, 71 top, 71 bottom, 72–73, 73 right, 74, 75 top, 77, 79, 80, 82–83, 84, 85, 86 top, 86 bottom, 87, 90 top, 90 bottom, 91, 93 right, 94, 95, 96 bottom, 97, 98, 99, 102 top, 102 bottom, 103, 104–105, 106 top, 106 bottom, 107, 108–109

Hans Halberstadt Collection: pp. 9, 11 bottom, 13, 14 top, 24 inset, 27 bottom, 29 right, 42 bottom, 46, 49 bottom, 51 bottom, 62, 65 bottom, 75 bottom, 76, 81, 96 top

©Thomas V. Labash: pp. 14 bottom, 78, 92–93, 101 inset

Private Collection: pp. 11 top, 15, 30, 38, 39, 70

©David Schiefelbein: pp. 100–101

Digital retouching, Daniel J. Rutkowski: pp.9, 65